# The Forcefield:

## Psalm 91 Revealed

Jeremy Lopez

The Forcefield: Psalm 91 Revealed

Published by Dr. Jeremy Lopez

Copyright © 2023

# ENDORSEMENTS

*Jeremy does an excellent job of giving balanced instruction on how to meditate, and also explaining the benefits that come from having a regular meditation and mindfulness practice. I love how Jeremy is not afraid to learn from and quote those outside the Christian tradition. He is able to explain the ancient concepts simply from a Biblical perspective.* – Kari Browning, Director, *The Beautiful Revolution*

*You are put on this earth with incredible potential and a divine destiny. This powerful, practical man shows you how to tap into power you did not even know you had.* – Brian Tracy – Author, *The Power of Self Confidence*

*I found myself savoring the concepts of the Law of Attraction merging with the Law of Creativity until slowly the beautiful truths seeped deeper into my thirsty soul. I am called to be a Creator! My friend, Dr. Jeremy Lopez, has a way of reminding us of our eternal 'I-Am-ness' while putting the tools in our hands to unlock our endless creative potential with the Divine mind. As a musical composer, I am excited to explore, with greater understanding, the infinite realm of possibilities as I place fingers on my piano and whisper, 'Let there be!'* – Dony McGuire, Grammy Award winning artist and musical composer

*Jeremy dives deep into the power of consciousness and shows us that we can create a world where the champion within us can shine and how we can manifest our desires to live a life of fulfillment. A must read!* – Greg S. Reid – *Forbes* and *Inc.* top rated Keynote Speaker

*I have been privileged to know Jeremy Lopez for many years, as well as sharing the platform with him at a number of conferences. Through this time, I have found him as a man of integrity, commitment, wisdom, and one of the most networked people I have met. Jeremy is an entrepreneur and a leader of leaders. He has amazing insights into leadership competencies and values. He has a passion to ignite this latent potential within individuals and organizations and provide ongoing development and coaching to bring about competitive advantage and success. I would highly recommend him as a speaker, coach, mentor, and consultant.* – Chris Gaborit – Learning Leader, Trainer

*Dr. Jeremy Lopez's book Universal Laws: Are They Biblical? is a breath of fresh air and much needed to answer the questions that people have been asking about the correlation between Biblical and Universal Laws. I have known Jeremy Lopez for years, and as a Biblical scholar, he gives an in-depth explanation and understanding of the perfect blending and merging into the secrets and mysteries of these miraculous Laws and how Bible-based the Universal Laws truly are. As the show host for the past twelve years on The Law of Attraction Radio Network, this book answers questions that I have received from Christian and spiritual seekers around the globe about the relationship between the metaphysical and Biblical truths.*

*After reading this book, readers will feel empowered and have strong faith that God has indeed given us these Bible-based Universal and Divine Laws to tap into so that we can live and create an abundant life.* – Constance Arnold, M.A., Author, Speaker, Professional Counselor, Host of *The Think, Believe & Manifest Talk Show*

# TABLE OF CONTENTS

Preface                         p.1

Introduction                    p.17

God's Ultimate Protection       p.37

Zoe                             p.61

Song of Protection              p.79

Contributing to the Plan        p.97

Intimacy                        p.117

God in All Things               p.141

Positioning                     p.159

Sufficient Grace                p.179

Understanding Secret Places     p.195

The Angelic Realms              p.209

# Preface

You are now alone. Not once have you ever been left to face life alone. And not only are you never alone, you are safe. You are protected. God has you covered.

Have you ever felt like you were all alone, going through life's challenges on your own? It's a common feeling, but I'm here to remind you that you're not alone at all. In fact, there's someone who's been looking out for you since the day you were born - God. Yes, that's right. God is always protecting us, even when we don't realize it. It's easy to get caught up in the struggles and hardships of life and forget that we have a divine protector watching over us.

But if we take a step back and look at the bigger picture, we can see the ways in which God has been guiding us all along.

Think about the times when things could have gone wrong, but didn't. Maybe you narrowly avoided a car accident, or you missed a flight that ended up crashing. These moments might seem like luck or coincidence, but they could also be the work of a higher power looking out for you.

God's protection isn't just limited to physical safety, either. He also watches over us emotionally and spiritually. When we're going through a tough time, God is there to comfort us and guide us towards the light. He gives us the strength to get through our struggles and come out stronger on the other side.

Of course, it's easy to question God's protection when things aren't going well. We might wonder why God would allow us to go through difficult times if he's really watching over us. But the truth is, God's protection isn't about preventing us from experiencing hardships - it's about helping us through them. When we face challenges, we have the opportunity to grow and learn. We become stronger, wiser, and more compassionate. And throughout it all, God is there to guide us and protect us. He's always watching over us, even when we don't realize it.

So if you ever feel alone or lost, remember that God is always with you. He's protecting you, guiding you, and helping you through life's ups and downs. All you have to do is trust in him, and he'll never let you down.

God's protection doesn't mean that we won't face challenges or difficult times. Life is full of ups and downs, and we all have to go through struggles and hardships at some point. But

God's protection means that we are never alone in those moments. He is always with us, giving us the strength to persevere and overcome.

In the Bible, there are countless examples of God's protection. The story of Daniel in the lion's den is a perfect example. Despite being thrown into a pit of hungry lions, God protected Daniel and kept him safe. Similarly, in the story of Shadrach, Meshach, and Abednego, God protected them from the fiery furnace and allowed them to emerge unscathed.

These stories might seem like ancient history, but the truth is, God's protection is just as real today as it was back then. We might not be facing lions or fiery furnaces, but we still need God's protection in our daily lives. Whether we're dealing with health problems, financial struggles, or relationship issues, God is always there to guide us and protect us.

One of the most beautiful things about God's protection is that it's available to everyone, regardless of our beliefs or backgrounds. God doesn't discriminate based on race, gender, or social status. He loves us all equally and wants to protect us all.

So if you ever feel like you're facing life's challenges on your own, remember that you have a divine protector watching over you. All you have to do is open your heart and trust in God's plan for you. He has a plan for your life, and it's a good one. With God's protection, you can overcome any obstacle and achieve anything you set your mind to.

Another important aspect of God's protection is the peace it brings to our lives. When we know that we are under God's protection, we can rest assured that we are safe and secure. We can have peace in the midst of chaos and find comfort in the midst of uncertainty.

God's protection also helps us to navigate life's challenges with wisdom and discernment. When we trust in God's guidance, we can make better decisions and avoid unnecessary risks. We can also have confidence that God will lead us down the right path, even when we don't know what the future holds.

Of course, trusting in God's protection isn't always easy. It requires faith and a willingness to let go of our own control. It means acknowledging that we can't do everything on our own and that we need God's help. But when we take that step of faith, we open ourselves up to a world of possibilities and opportunities.

Take comfort in the fact that God is always protecting you. Trust in his plan for your life and have faith that he will guide you through whatever challenges you may face. With God's protection, you can live a life of peace, purpose, and fulfillment.

It's important to remember that God's protection extends beyond just our individual lives. God also protects us as a community and as a planet. He watches over the entire world, guiding us towards peace and harmony.

In times of natural disasters or global crises, it can be easy to feel like God has abandoned us. But the truth is, he is always with us, even in the midst of chaos. We may not always understand why things happen the way they do, but we can trust that God is in control and working towards a greater purpose.

When we come together as a community and trust in God's protection, we can overcome even the most daunting challenges. We can work towards a brighter future and create a world that is filled with love, compassion, and understanding.

God's protection also extends to our spiritual lives. He watches over us as we grow in our faith, guiding us towards a deeper understanding of his love and grace. He protects us from the negative influences of the world and helps us to stay on the path of righteousness.

Ultimately, God's protection is a reminder of his unending love for us. He wants nothing but the best for us and will go to great lengths to protect us from harm. When we trust in God's protection, we can live our lives with confidence and courage, knowing that we are never alone.

In addition to protecting us, God also gives us free will. We have the ability to make our own choices and shape our own lives. While this may seem like a contradiction to God's protection, it's important to remember that God's protection isn't about controlling our every move. It's about guiding us towards the best possible outcomes while allowing us to learn and grow from our experiences.

Sometimes, God's protection may not look the way we expect it to. We may experience pain or hardship, but in the end, these challenges can help us to become stronger and more resilient. We may not understand why things happen the way they do, but we can trust that God has a plan for our lives and that he is always working towards our greater good.

Remember that God is always protecting you, even if it doesn't feel like it. Trust in his plan for your life and have faith that he will guide you through whatever challenges you may face. With God's protection, you can overcome anything and live a life of peace, purpose, and fulfillment.

Do you believe in angels? While some people might dismiss them as mere myth or legend, others believe that angels are real beings sent by God to watch over us and protect us from harm.

Angels are often depicted as beautiful, winged creatures with halos, but in reality, they can take on many different forms. They may appear as humans, animals, or even as a whisper in our hearts. Regardless of their form, angels are always present, watching over us and guiding us towards the light.

So how do we know that angels are real? Well, for starters, there are countless stories of people who have experienced the presence of angels in their lives. Some have even reported seeing or hearing from angels during moments of crisis or danger.

But even if you've never had a direct encounter with an angel, there are still many signs that they are watching over you. Maybe you've experienced a sudden sense of peace or comfort during a difficult time, or perhaps you've had a close call that could have ended much worse. These could be signs that angels are working behind the scenes to protect you.

It's important to note that angels aren't just protectors in times of physical danger. They also watch over us emotionally and spiritually, providing comfort and guidance when we need it most. Whether we're going through a tough time, feeling lost or alone, or simply in need of inspiration, angels are always there to help us.

Of course, it can be easy to dismiss the idea of angels as just wishful thinking. But when we open our hearts and minds to the possibility of their existence, we can start to see the ways in which they are working in our lives. We can begin to trust in their guidance and protection, knowing that we are never alone.

So the next time you're feeling scared or uncertain, remember that angels are always with you. They are watching over you, protecting you, and guiding you towards the light. All you have to do is have faith and trust in their presence. With the help of angels, you can overcome any obstacle and live a life filled with love, peace, and purpose.

Angels are often associated with a sense of divine guidance and wisdom. They have been known to provide us with clarity and direction when we're feeling lost or confused. Sometimes, they may even send us messages through signs or symbols to help us navigate our way through life.

It's important to note that angels aren't just present in times of need or crisis. They also celebrate our successes and accomplishments, and are there to share in our joy and happiness. They encourage us to pursue our dreams and to always strive for our highest potential.

One of the most beautiful things about angels is that they are always available to us. We don't need to pray or make a special request for their help - they are always watching over us, ready to provide us with guidance and protection at any moment. All we need to do is open our hearts and minds to their presence, and be willing to receive their love and support.

In times when we feel like the world is against us, it's comforting to know that angels are always by our side. They are our protectors, our confidants, and our biggest cheerleaders. With their help, we can overcome any obstacle and achieve our greatest dreams.

If you're feeling lost, scared, or uncertain, take comfort in the knowledge that angels are always watching over you. Trust in their guidance and protection, and know that you are never alone. With their help, you can navigate life's challenges with grace and ease, and live a life filled with purpose and joy.

The idea of angels protecting us can bring a sense of peace and comfort in times of turmoil. It can help us to feel a deeper connection to a higher power and to trust that there is a divine plan for our lives.

When we believe in the existence of angels, it can also inspire us to be more kind, compassionate, and loving towards others. After all, if there are beings dedicated to watching over us and protecting us, shouldn't we also do our part to watch over and protect others?

There are many ways to connect with the energy of angels and invite their presence into our lives. Some people like to meditate or pray, while others may use crystals or angel cards as a way of connecting with their energy. There is no one "right" way to connect with angels - the most important thing is to be open and receptive to their guidance and support.

It's also important to remember that while angels can offer us guidance and protection, they don't interfere with our free will. We still have the power to make our own choices and create our own paths in life. However, by inviting the presence of angels into our lives, we can make better decisions and feel more supported on our journey.

If you're looking for a sense of comfort, guidance, or protection, consider connecting with the energy of angels. Trust in their presence, and know that they are always watching over you, offering you love, guidance, and protection every step of the way. With their help, you can navigate life's challenges with grace and ease, and live a life filled with purpose and joy. May this book serve as a testament to the help that exists just beyond the veil.

# Introduction

It is one of the most popular, most talked about passages of scripture and one that continues to inspire us and cause our faith to rise. I am speaking of Psalm 91. However, as you will see, there are so many intricate and detailed layers of revelation existing within the passage which share more than just a theme of protection. As you read *The Forcefield: Psalm 91 Revealed*, may you realize just how safe you are in the Presence of God and may you encounter a new level of closeness with the Holy Spirit.

He that dwelleth in the secret place of the most High shall abide under the shadow of the Almighty.

I will say of the LORD, He is my refuge and my fortress: my God; in him will I trust.

Surely he shall deliver thee from the snare of the fowler, and from the noisome pestilence.

He shall cover thee with his feathers, and under his wings shalt thou trust: his truth shall be thy shield and buckler.

Thou shalt not be afraid for the terror by night; nor for the arrow that flieth by day;

Nor for the pestilence that walketh in darkness; nor for the destruction that wasteth at noonday.

A thousand shall fall at thy side, and ten thousand at thy right hand; but it shall not come nigh thee.

Only with thine eyes shalt thou behold and see the reward of the wicked.

Because thou hast made the LORD, which is my refuge, even the most High, thy habitation;

There shall no evil befall thee, neither shall any plague come nigh thy dwelling.

For he shall give his angels charge over thee, to keep thee in all thy ways.

They shall bear thee up in their hands, lest thou dash thy foot against a stone.

Thou shalt tread upon the lion and adder: the young lion and the dragon shalt thou trample under feet.

Because he hath set his love upon me, therefore will I deliver him: I will set him on high, because he hath known my name.

He shall call upon me, and I will answer him: I will be with him in trouble; I will deliver him, and honour him.

With long life will I satisfy him, and shew him my salvation. (Psalm 91:1-16 KJV)

In many cultures and religions, the idea of a divine power or God protecting and guiding our lives is a common belief. Regardless of your specific beliefs, the concept of a higher power watching over us and offering protection can bring a sense of comfort and security. In this post, we will explore the concept of God's protection in our lives and how it can impact our daily existence.

One of the most fundamental beliefs of many religions is that God is omnipotent and omniscient, meaning that God is all-powerful and all-knowing. This belief leads to the idea that God is able to protect and guide us in all aspects of our lives. Whether we are facing physical danger, emotional turmoil, or spiritual struggles, God can provide a sense of safety and security.

Many people who believe in God's protection feel that they have a personal relationship with God. They believe that God is always present in their lives, guiding them and protecting them from harm. This belief can help individuals feel less alone and more supported, even in difficult times.

The idea of God's protection can also offer a sense of peace and calm. When we feel anxious or stressed, turning to our faith and trusting in God's protection can help us feel more grounded and centered. It can remind us that we are not in control of everything, and that we can rely on a higher power to guide us through life's challenges.

Another important aspect of God's protection is the belief that it extends beyond this life. Many religious traditions believe in an afterlife, and that God's protection continues beyond our physical existence. This belief can offer comfort to those who are grieving, and help individuals feel more hopeful about the future.

Of course, the idea of God's protection can also raise questions and doubts for some individuals. For example, if God is all-powerful and all-knowing, why do bad things happen to good people? While there are no easy answers to these questions, many people believe that God's protection does not necessarily mean that we will never face hardship or suffering. Rather, it means that God is with us, guiding us and helping us to find strength and resilience in the face of adversity.

The concept of God's protection is an important aspect of many religious beliefs. Whether you believe in a specific deity or simply in the idea of a higher power, trusting in God's protection can bring a sense of comfort, peace, and security to your life. It can help you feel less alone and more supported, even in difficult times, and remind you that there is always hope and guidance available to you.

While God's protection can offer comfort and support, it's important to remember that it doesn't necessarily mean that we won't face challenges or difficulties in life. Instead, it means that we have a source of strength and guidance to help us navigate those challenges.

One way that people may experience God's protection is through prayer. Prayer is a way of communicating with God and expressing our needs and desires. Through prayer, we can ask for God's protection and guidance, and trust that our prayers will be heard.

Another way that people may experience God's protection is through acts of kindness and compassion. Many religious traditions emphasize the importance of treating others with love and kindness, and believe that doing so can bring blessings and protection. When we show compassion and generosity to others, we may feel a sense of fulfillment and purpose, as well as a sense of protection from God.

It's also worth noting that God's protection doesn't necessarily mean that we will always get what we want or avoid all harm. Sometimes, we may face difficult or painful experiences that we don't understand. However, trusting in God's protection can help us find meaning and purpose in those experiences, and allow us to grow and learn from them.

Ultimately, the idea of God's protection is a deeply personal and individual belief. While some people may experience it in a more tangible way, others may find comfort in simply knowing that there is a higher power watching over them. Regardless of how we experience God's protection, it can offer a sense of comfort, security, and hope in a world that can often feel uncertain and chaotic.

In addition to prayer and acts of kindness, many people may find that practicing their faith helps them feel a sense of God's protection. This can include attending religious services, reading scripture, and participating in spiritual practices such as meditation or yoga. By engaging in these practices, we may feel more connected to

God and more aware of the ways in which God is guiding and protecting us.

Another way that people may experience God's protection is through the support of a faith community. Many religious traditions emphasize the importance of coming together as a community to support one another and strengthen our faith. By being part of a community of believers, we can find comfort and strength in our shared beliefs and experiences, and feel a sense of protection and guidance from God.

It's also worth noting that God's protection can take many forms. For example, it may manifest as a sudden change in circumstances that leads us to a better outcome, or as a sense of peace and calm during a difficult time. It's important to be open to these different forms of protection, and to trust that God is always working in our lives, even if we don't always see it.

At the same time, it's important to remember that God's protection doesn't mean that we should be reckless or ignore potential dangers. We still need to take reasonable precautions to protect ourselves and others. However, by trusting in God's protection, we can approach life with a sense of courage and resilience, knowing that we are never truly alone and that there is always a source of guidance and support available to us.

The concept of God's protection is a powerful and meaningful belief for many people. By trusting in God's protection, we can find comfort and strength in difficult times, and approach life with a sense of hope and purpose. While the form that God's protection takes may vary from person to person, the belief in a

27

higher power guiding and protecting our lives can offer a profound sense of meaning and security.

It's also important to note that the belief in God's protection is not limited to any specific religion or culture. Many people from different backgrounds and belief systems may find comfort in the idea that there is a higher power watching over them and offering protection.

Furthermore, the belief in God's protection can be especially powerful during times of crisis or uncertainty. When we face situations that are beyond our control, such as a natural disaster or a personal loss, the idea of God's protection can help us find the strength and resilience to move forward. By trusting in God's protection, we can find hope and meaning in even the darkest of times.

Another important aspect of the belief in God's protection is the idea that we are not alone in our struggles. When we trust in God's protection, we can feel a sense of connection to something greater than ourselves, and find comfort in the knowledge that others share our beliefs and experiences. This sense of community and connection can be a powerful source of support and encouragement.

Ultimately, the belief in God's protection can offer a sense of peace and security in a world that can often feel chaotic and unpredictable. By trusting in a higher power to guide and protect us, we can find the strength and courage to face life's challenges with hope and resilience. Whether through prayer, spiritual practices, or simply a deep sense of faith, the belief in God's protection can offer a profound sense of meaning and purpose in our lives.

Psalm 91 is a powerful and inspiring passage found in the Bible. It is known as the "Psalm of Protection" and is often read during times of difficulty and uncertainty. In this post, we will explore the meaning and significance of Psalm 91 and how it can offer comfort and hope to those in need.

The Psalm begins with the following words: "He who dwells in the secret place of the Most High shall abide under the shadow of the Almighty." This verse sets the tone for the entire passage, emphasizing the idea of finding refuge and protection in God. The imagery of dwelling in the "secret place" and being under the "shadow" of God highlights the sense of safety and security that comes from being close to God.

The Psalm goes on to describe the various ways in which God offers protection to those who trust in Him. It speaks of protection from "the snare of the fowler" and "the deadly pestilence," as well as protection from "the terror by night" and "the arrow that flies by day." These images speak to the various dangers and challenges we may face in life, and emphasize the idea that God is with us through it all.

The Psalm also speaks of God's faithfulness and loyalty to those who trust in Him. It says, "Because he has set his love upon Me, therefore I will deliver him; I will set him on high, because he has known My name. He shall call upon Me, and I will answer him; I will be with him in trouble; I will deliver him and honor him." These verses highlight the idea that God is not only our protector, but also our ally and friend.

The Psalm ends with a declaration of faith and trust in God. It says, "With long life I will satisfy him, and show him My salvation." This verse speaks to the idea of finding ultimate fulfillment and salvation in God, and emphasizes the importance of trusting in Him completely.

Psalm 91 is a powerful and uplifting passage that speaks to the idea of finding refuge and protection in God. It reminds us that we are not alone in our struggles, and that God is with us through all the challenges and difficulties we may face in life. By placing our trust in God and seeking refuge in His love and protection, we can find comfort and hope, and ultimately experience the fulfillment and salvation that comes from a deep and abiding faith in Him.

One of the most striking aspects of Psalm 91 is the imagery it uses to convey the idea of God's protection. The Psalm speaks of being hidden under God's wings, of being shielded by His faithfulness and truth, and of having His angels guard and protect us. These images convey a sense of God's powerful presence in our lives, and highlight the idea that He is actively working to keep us safe and secure.

Another important theme in Psalm 91 is the idea of trust. Throughout the Psalm, the speaker expresses their unwavering faith in God's protection and provision, even in the face of danger and uncertainty. This theme of trust is an important one in many religious traditions, as it speaks to the idea of surrendering control and placing our faith in a higher power. By trusting in God's protection, we can find a sense of peace and security, knowing that we are not alone in our struggles.

It's also worth noting that the Psalm doesn't promise a life free from hardship or difficulty. Rather, it acknowledges that we may face danger and adversity, but emphasizes the idea that God is with us through it all. By placing our trust in Him, we can find the strength and resilience to face life's challenges with courage and hope.

In addition to its spiritual significance, Psalm 91 has also been used in a number of practical ways throughout history. For example, during World War II, it was often read as a source of comfort and hope for soldiers and civilians alike. In more recent times, it has been used as a basis for prayers of protection during times of natural disaster or political turmoil.

Ultimately, Psalm 91 offers a message of hope and comfort for anyone who may be feeling lost or uncertain. By turning to God and seeking His protection and provision, we can find the strength and resilience to face whatever challenges come our way. As the Psalm says,

"He shall call upon Me, and I will answer him; I will be with him in trouble; I will deliver him and honor him." By placing our trust in God's protection, we can find the courage to face life's challenges with faith and hope.

God's Ultimate Protection

The Bible is filled with promises of divine protection for those who fear God. This is a theme that runs throughout both the Old and New Testaments, and is one that brings great comfort and reassurance to believers.

To understand how the Bible teaches divine protection, we must first understand what it means to fear God. In the Bible, the fear of God is not a sense of terror or dread, but rather a deep reverence and respect for God's power and authority. It is an acknowledgement of God's sovereignty over all things, and a recognition that we are dependent on Him for our well-being.

One of the most well-known passages in the Bible that speaks to divine protection for those who fear God is Psalm 91. This psalm is a beautiful expression of the believer's trust in God's care and protection. It begins with these words:

"He who dwells in the shelter of the Most High

will abide in the shadow of the Almighty.

I will say to the Lord, 'My refuge and my fortress,

my God, in whom I trust.'"

The psalm goes on to describe the many ways in which God protects His people:

"He will deliver you from the snare of the fowler

and from the deadly pestilence.

He will cover you with his pinions,

and under his wings you will find refuge;

his faithfulness is a shield and buckler."


"You will not fear the terror of the night,

nor the arrow that flies by day,

nor the pestilence that stalks in darkness,

nor the destruction that wastes at noonday."


"Because he holds fast to me in love, I will deliver him;

I will protect him, because he knows my name."

The message of Psalm 91 is clear: those who trust in God and fear Him will be protected from harm. This does not mean that believers will never face difficulties or challenges in life, but it does mean that God will be with them through those trials and will ultimately deliver them from harm.

Another passage in the Bible that speaks to divine protection is Proverbs 18:10, which says:

"The name of the Lord is a strong tower;

the righteous man runs into it and is safe."

This verse emphasizes the idea that God is a refuge for His people. Just as a tower provides protection from enemies, so too does God provide protection for those who seek Him. The righteous can take comfort in the fact that God is a place of safety and security for them.

In the New Testament, we see the idea of divine protection continued in the teachings of Jesus. In Matthew 10:28-31, Jesus tells His disciples:

"Do not fear those who kill the body but cannot kill the soul. Rather fear him who can destroy both soul and body in hell. Are not two sparrows sold for a penny? And not one of them will fall to the ground apart from your Father. But even the hairs of your head are all numbered. Fear not, therefore; you are of more value than many sparrows."

Here, Jesus is reassuring His followers that even in the face of persecution and suffering, God is with them and will protect them. He reminds them that they are of great value to God, and that He cares for even the smallest details of their lives.

The Bible teaches that there is divine protection for those who fear God. This protection is not a guarantee that believers will never face difficulties or challenges, but it is a promise that God will be with them through those trials and will ultimately deliver them from harm. As believers, we can take great comfort in the fact that God is our refuge and our fortress, and that He is always watching over us.

In addition to the specific verses and passages mentioned above, there are many other examples throughout the Bible of God's protection for those who fear Him. For instance, in Psalm 34:7, we read that "The angel of the Lord encamps around those who fear him, and delivers them." This verse suggests that God sends His angels to protect and defend His people.

Similarly, in Isaiah 43:2, God says, "When you pass through the waters, I will be with you; and through the rivers, they shall not overwhelm you; when you walk through fire you shall not be burned, and the flame shall not consume you." This verse portrays God's protection as all-encompassing, covering every aspect of our lives and providing us with strength and courage in the face of adversity.

Throughout the Bible, we also see examples of individuals who experienced God's protection firsthand. For example, in the story of Daniel in the lions' den (Daniel 6), we see how God protected Daniel from harm despite his enemies' attempts to harm him. Similarly, in the story of Shadrach, Meshach, and Abednego in the fiery furnace (Daniel 3), we see how God miraculously saved these men from certain death. These stories serve as powerful reminders that God's protection is not just a theoretical concept, but a real and tangible experience for those who put their trust in Him.

It's important to note that the promise of divine protection is not a license for recklessness or foolishness. Rather, it's a reminder that even in the midst of danger and uncertainty, we can trust in God's provision and care for us. As Proverbs 21:31 says, "The horse is made ready for the day of battle, but the victory belongs to the Lord." While we may take practical steps to protect ourselves, ultimately it is God who provides the victory and the protection we need.

The Bible teaches that there is divine protection for those who fear God. This protection is not a guarantee of a trouble-free life, but rather a promise that God is with us through every trial and that He will ultimately deliver us from harm. As we put our trust in Him and seek to live in reverence and awe of His power and goodness, we can rest assured that He will be our refuge and our shield, now and forevermore.

It's also worth noting that the promise of divine protection is not just limited to physical harm or danger. God's protection extends to all areas of our lives, including our emotional, mental, and spiritual well-being.

In Psalm 23, one of the most well-known passages in the Bible, we see a beautiful expression of God's protection and care for His people. The psalm begins, "The Lord is my shepherd; I shall not want. He makes me lie down in green pastures. He leads me beside still waters. He restores my soul."

These verses paint a picture of a caring and attentive shepherd who provides for the needs of his sheep. The imagery of green pastures and still waters suggests a place of safety and security, where the sheep can rest and be refreshed. And the phrase "He restores my soul" speaks to God's ability to heal and renew us in every area of our lives.

Throughout the psalm, we see how God protects and guides His people, even in the midst of danger or difficulty. In verse 4, the psalmist says, "Even though I walk through the valley of the shadow of death, I will fear no evil, for you are with me; your rod and your staff, they comfort me." This verse reminds us that God is with us even in the darkest moments of our lives, and that His presence brings comfort and peace.

Ultimately, the promise of divine protection is rooted in God's character and His unwavering love for His people. As Romans 8:38-39 says, "For I am sure that neither death nor life, nor angels nor rulers, nor things present nor things to come, nor powers, nor height nor depth, nor anything else in all creation, will be able to separate us from the love of God in Christ Jesus our Lord." This verse assures us that no matter what we may face in life, God's love and protection will never fail us.

The Bible teaches that there is divine protection for those who fear God. This protection is not just limited to physical harm or danger, but extends to all areas of our lives. As we put our trust in God and seek to live in reverence and awe of His power and goodness, we can rest assured that He will be our refuge and our strength, now and forevermore.

The promise of divine protection is not just a one-time event or a momentary experience, but a continuous reality for those who fear God. It is a promise that is reinforced and affirmed throughout the Bible, in both the Old and New Testaments.

For example, in Isaiah 54:17, God declares, "No weapon that is fashioned against you shall succeed, and you shall refute every tongue that rises against you in judgment. This is the heritage of the servants of the Lord and their vindication from me, declares the Lord." This verse reminds us that God is always on our side, fighting for us and protecting us from harm.

In the New Testament, we see a similar theme of divine protection in the teachings of Jesus. In John 10:27-28, Jesus says, "My sheep hear my voice, and I know them, and they follow me. I give them eternal life, and they will never perish, and no one will snatch them out of my hand." This verse emphasizes the idea of God's protection as a permanent and unbreakable reality for those who belong to Him.

Another example of divine protection in the New Testament is found in 2 Timothy 4:18, where Paul writes, "The Lord will rescue me from every evil deed and bring me safely into his heavenly kingdom. To him be the glory forever and ever. Amen." This verse highlights the idea of God's protection as a means of bringing us safely into His kingdom, both in this life and in the life to come.

The promise of divine protection is not just a theoretical concept, but a reality that many believers have experienced firsthand. Throughout history, there have been countless stories of individuals who have faced incredible danger or persecution, yet have been miraculously protected by God.

For example, in the early church, there were many instances of believers being thrown into prison or facing execution for their faith. Yet time and time again, God provided miraculous escapes or interventions that spared their lives.

These stories serve as powerful reminders of God's faithfulness and His unwavering commitment to protecting His people.

The promise of divine protection for those who fear God is a central theme throughout the Bible. It is a promise that provides comfort, strength, and reassurance to believers in every circumstance of life. As we put our trust in God and seek to live in reverence and awe of His power and goodness, we can rest assured that He will be our refuge and our shield, now and forevermore.

Divine protection is tied to divine destiny. The concept of destiny is one that has fascinated and intrigued people for centuries. It is the idea that each of us has a specific purpose or calling that we must fulfill in our lives, and that this purpose is predetermined by God.

In the Bible, we see many examples of individuals who were called by God to fulfill a specific destiny. For instance, Moses was called to lead the Israelites out of slavery in Egypt. David was called to be king of Israel. Paul was called to be an apostle to the Gentiles.

These individuals didn't choose their destinies; rather, their destinies chose them. They were each uniquely equipped and empowered by God to carry out the tasks that He had set before them.

But it's not just these biblical figures who have destinies in God. Each and every one of us has a destiny that we must carry out. Ephesians 2:10 says, "For we are his workmanship, created in Christ Jesus for good works, which God prepared beforehand, that we should walk in them." This verse reminds us that we are not accidents or mistakes, but rather we were created by God for a specific purpose.

So how do we discover our destiny in God? The first step is to seek Him and His will for our lives. This means spending time in prayer, reading the Bible, and seeking wise counsel from other believers. As we seek God's guidance, He will begin to reveal His plan and purpose for our lives.

Another important aspect of discovering our destiny is to use the gifts and talents that God has given us. Each of us has been uniquely gifted by God, and He wants us to use those gifts to bring glory to Him and to bless others. 1 Peter 4:10 says, "As each has received a gift, use it to serve one another, as good stewards of God's varied grace."

When we use our gifts and talents to serve others, we are fulfilling our destiny in God. We are using the abilities that He has given us to make a positive impact on the world around us.

But discovering and fulfilling our destiny is not always easy. There may be obstacles and challenges along the way. We may face doubts, fears, or insecurities that hold us back from fully embracing God's plan for our lives.

That's why it's important to remember that we don't fulfill our destinies in our own strength. Rather, we rely on God's strength and guidance to see us through. Philippians 4:13 says, "I can do all things through him who strengthens me." When we rely on God's strength, we can overcome any obstacle or challenge that comes our way.

We all have destinies in God that we must carry out. Our destinies are not predetermined by our own choices or actions, but rather by God's plan and purpose for our lives. As we seek Him and use the gifts and talents that He has given us, we can fulfill our destinies and make a positive impact on the world around us. And as we rely on God's strength and guidance, we can overcome any obstacle that comes our way.

When we discover and begin to pursue our destinies in God, we may find that it requires us to step out of our comfort zones and take risks. We may be called to do things that seem impossible or difficult, but with God's help, we can accomplish them.

One of the most important things to remember when pursuing our destinies in God is to stay connected to Him. This means continuing to seek His guidance, spending time in prayer, and maintaining a close relationship with Him. As we do so, we can be confident that we are on the right path and that He will continue to lead and guide us.

Another important aspect of fulfilling our destinies is to be patient and trust in God's timing. We may have a sense of what our destiny is, but it may take time for God to fully reveal His plan to us. We may also encounter setbacks or delays along the way. But we can trust that God is always working behind the scenes, and that He will bring His plans to fruition in His perfect timing.

It's also important to remember that our destinies in God are not just about accomplishing great things or achieving success in the world's eyes. Our destinies are ultimately about glorifying God and bringing Him honor and praise. When we pursue our destinies with this mindset, we can be confident that we are on the right path, regardless of the outcome.

It's important to recognize that our destinies in God are not just individual pursuits, but are also intertwined with the destinies of others. God often calls us to work together with others to accomplish His purposes in the world. This means being willing to serve and support others, even when it may be difficult or inconvenient.

Our destinies in God are a central aspect of our lives as believers. When we seek God's guidance and use the gifts and talents that He has given us, we can fulfill our destinies and make a positive impact on the world around us. But we must also be patient, trust in God's timing, and remember that our destinies are ultimately about bringing glory to Him. And as we work together with others to accomplish His purposes, we can be confident that we are fulfilling His plan for our lives.

There is also angelic help for them that fear God. The concept of angels has been a part of human belief systems for millennia. In many religions and spiritual traditions, angels are seen as messengers or helpers from a higher power. In Christianity, angels are believed to be powerful spiritual beings who serve as God's messengers and agents of protection and guidance.

The Bible is full of references to angels and their role in God's plan for humanity. From the story of Jacob's ladder in Genesis to the visions of angels in the book of Revelation, we see that angels have been a part of God's plan for humanity from the beginning.

One of the most powerful and reassuring aspects of the concept of angels is the idea that there is always angelic help behind the scenes. Even when we may feel alone or overwhelmed, we can be confident that there are angels working on our behalf, protecting us and guiding us towards God's will for our lives.

In Psalm 91:11-12, we read, "For he will command his angels concerning you to guard you in all your ways. On their hands they will bear you up, lest you strike your foot against a stone." This verse highlights the idea that angels are always working to protect us, even in the midst of danger or uncertainty.

Similarly, in Hebrews 1:14, we read that angels are "ministering spirits sent out to serve for the sake of those who are to inherit salvation." This verse reminds us that angels are actively working to help us in our spiritual journey, guiding us towards salvation and eternal life with God.

But the role of angels is not just limited to protection and guidance. Throughout the Bible, we see examples of angels intervening in miraculous ways, performing feats that seem impossible to human beings. From the angel who delivered Peter from prison in Acts 12 to the angels who announced the birth of Jesus in Luke 2, we see that angels are capable of incredible acts of power and intervention.

The idea of angelic help behind the scenes is not just a theoretical concept, but a reality that many believers have experienced firsthand. There are countless stories of people who have been saved from danger or harm by what they believe was angelic intervention. Others have reported experiencing a sense of peace and comfort in times of distress, which they attribute to the presence of angels.

The concept of angelic help behind the scenes is a powerful and reassuring aspect of the Christian faith. It reminds us that we are never alone, and that there are powerful spiritual beings working on our behalf to protect us and guide us towards God's will for our lives. As we put our trust in God and seek to live in obedience to His commands, we can be confident that there is always angelic help behind the scenes, working to bring about His purposes in our lives.

# Zoe

When we align ourselves to the plans and to the purposes of God, we become more able to see the hand of God in operation within our lives. We become more able to see just how God protects us. Uncovering Psalm 91, we find that there is refuge and safety in the "shadows" of the Almighty. This refers to a secret place of deeper intimacy with God.

The Bible teaches that there are two types of life: bios and zoe. Bios refers to physical life, which is temporary and subject to decay, while zoe refers to eternal life, which is spiritual and never fades away. Zoe life is a central theme of the Bible and is often referred to as the "abundant life" or the "life to the full." It is the kind of life that Jesus came to give us, and it is available to all who believe in him.

According to the Bible, zoe life is characterized by several key elements. First and foremost, it is a life that is rooted in a personal relationship with God. This relationship is made possible through faith in Jesus Christ, who is the way, the truth, and the life.

Zoe life is also marked by freedom from sin and death. The Bible teaches that sin is the root of all human suffering and that the wages of sin is death. But through Jesus Christ, we can be set free from the power of sin and death and experience the fullness of zoe life.

Another key element of zoe life is a deep sense of purpose and meaning. The Bible teaches that God has a unique plan for each of our lives and that when we walk in obedience to his will, we experience a sense of fulfillment and satisfaction that is beyond anything this world can offer.

Zoe life is also characterized by a sense of joy and peace that transcends our circumstances. This joy and peace come from knowing that our lives are in the hands of a loving and sovereign God who is working all things together for our good.

Zoe life is about living in the presence of God. The Bible teaches that in his presence there is fullness of joy and pleasures forevermore. It is a life that is marked by intimacy with God and a deep sense of awe and wonder at his goodness and grace.

The Bible teaches that zoe life is the abundant and eternal life that is available to all who believe in Jesus Christ. It is a life that is characterized by a personal relationship with

God, freedom from sin and death, a sense of purpose and meaning, joy and peace, and intimacy with God. May we all experience the fullness of zoe life as we walk in faith and obedience to him.

Zoe life is not just a future hope, but it is also a present reality that we can experience in our daily lives. It is a life that is lived in the power of the Holy Spirit, who dwells within us and empowers us to live a life that is pleasing to God.

The Holy Spirit enables us to love others with a selfless and sacrificial love, to serve others with humility and compassion, and to live a life of obedience to God's commands. As we walk in the Spirit, we bear the fruit of the Spirit, which is love, joy, peace, patience, kindness, goodness, faithfulness, gentleness, and self-control.

Zoe life is also a life of faith, where we trust in God's promises and rest in his provision. It is a life where we do not worry about tomorrow or the things of this world, but instead, we seek first his kingdom and his righteousness, knowing that he will take care of all our needs.

Furthermore, zoe life is a life of community, where we are united with other believers in Christ, sharing in each other's joys and burdens. It is a life where we bear one another's burdens, encourage one another, and build each other up in love.

Ultimately, zoe life finds its fulfillment in the future when we will be with Christ forever. It is a life that will never fade away, where we will experience the fullness of God's glory and be united with him and with one another.

The zoe life is not just a theological concept, but it is a reality that we can experience in our daily lives. It is a life that is characterized by a personal relationship with God, freedom from sin and death, a sense of purpose and meaning, joy and peace, intimacy with God, the power of the Holy Spirit, faith, community, and the hope of eternal life. May we all seek to live a life of zoe, knowing that it is the life that Jesus came to give us.

To fully embrace zoe life, we must be willing to surrender our will and our desires to God. We must lay down our old way of life, which is characterized by selfishness and sin, and put on the new self, which is created in the image of God.

This transformation is not something that we can do on our own, but it is the work of God in us. As we submit ourselves to him, he transforms us from the inside out, giving us new desires and empowering us to live a life that is pleasing to him.

Zoe life is also marked by a life of prayer and a commitment to God's Word. Through prayer, we can communicate with God and receive the guidance and strength that we need to live a life that is honoring to him. Through the study of his Word, we can come to know him more deeply and understand his will for our lives.

Moreover, zoe life is characterized by a life of mission, where we share the good news of Jesus Christ with others and make disciples of all nations. As we live out our faith and share the love of Christ with those around us, we become a witness to the transforming power of God in our lives.

Zoe life is a life of worship, where we give glory and honor to God in all that we do. As we recognize that all that we have and all that we are is a gift from him, we offer our lives as a living sacrifice, holy and pleasing to him.

Zoe life is a life that is characterized by a personal relationship with God, freedom from sin and death, a sense of purpose and meaning, joy and peace, intimacy with God, the power of the Holy Spirit, faith, community, the hope of eternal life, surrender, prayer, commitment to God's Word, mission, and worship. May we all seek to embrace zoe life and live a life that is pleasing to God.

One of the most significant aspects of zoe life is the transformation that takes place within us as we are renewed in our minds and hearts. This transformation is a process that occurs over time as we yield to the work of the Holy Spirit in our lives.

As we grow in our understanding of who God is and what he has done for us through Jesus

Christ, our perspective on life begins to change. We start to see things from an eternal perspective, and we recognize that the things of this world are temporary and fleeting.

This shift in perspective leads to a change in our values and priorities. We start to value the things that God values, such as love, justice, mercy, and compassion, and we prioritize the things that are important to him, such as worship, prayer, and serving others.

Another significant aspect of zoe life is the hope that we have in Christ. Even in the midst of the trials and difficulties of life, we can have confidence that God is working all things together for our good and that he has a plan and a purpose for our lives.

This hope is not just a wishful thinking or a positive attitude, but it is grounded in the reality of what God has done for us through Jesus

Christ. He has conquered sin and death, and he has promised to make all things new.

As we live out our lives in the hope of what is to come, we can be a light to those around us who are struggling and searching for meaning in life. We can offer them the hope that is found in Jesus Christ and share with them the transforming power of zoe life.

The zoe life is a life that is marked by transformation, hope, and a commitment to live according to God's values and priorities. May we all seek to embrace zoe life and allow the Holy Spirit to transform us from the inside out so that we may live a life that honors God and points others to Jesus Christ.

Another important aspect of zoe life is the power of forgiveness. As we receive God's forgiveness for our sins, we are also called to forgive others who have wronged us.

Forgiveness is not always easy, but it is necessary if we are to experience the fullness of zoe life. When we hold onto bitterness and resentment towards others, it not only harms our relationship with them, but it also hinders our relationship with God.

Forgiveness frees us from the bondage of bitterness and allows us to experience the joy and peace that comes from being reconciled to God and to others.

In addition to forgiveness, zoe life is also characterized by a life of generosity and giving. The Bible teaches that God loves a cheerful giver and that we are blessed to be a blessing to others.

When we live a life of generosity, we reflect the character of God, who has given us everything that we have. We also demonstrate our trust in

God's provision and our willingness to put the needs of others before our own.

Generosity is not just about giving money or material possessions, but it is also about giving of our time, talents, and resources to serve others and build up the body of Christ.

Furthermore, zoe life is a life of humility and submission to God's will. The Bible teaches that God opposes the proud but gives grace to the humble.

When we humble ourselves before God and submit to his will, we recognize that he is in control of our lives, and we trust him to guide us and direct us according to his purposes.

Zoe life is a life that is characterized by forgiveness, generosity, humility, and submission to God's will. May we all seek to live a life that reflects the character of God and brings glory to his name, as we embrace the abundant and eternal life that he has promised to us through Jesus Christ.

Another important aspect of zoe life is the call to love others as Christ has loved us. The Bible teaches that love is the greatest commandment and that we are to love God with all our heart, soul, mind, and strength, and to love our neighbor as ourselves.

Love is not just an emotion but is also an action that is demonstrated through our words and deeds. When we love others, we reflect the love of Christ, who gave his life for us while we were still sinners. In addition to love, zoe life is also characterized by a life of obedience to God's commands. The Bible teaches that if we love God, we will keep his commandments.

Obedience is not always easy, but it is necessary if we are to experience the fullness of zoe life. When we obey God's commands, we demonstrate our love for him and our trust in his wisdom and goodness.

Furthermore, zoe life is a life of faithfulness and perseverance. The Bible teaches that we are to run the race of faith with endurance and to press on towards the goal of the prize of the upward call of God in Christ Jesus.

Faithfulness and perseverance require us to trust in God's promises and to remain steadfast in our commitment to follow him, even when the road is difficult and the challenges are great.

Finally, zoe life is characterized by a life of praise and worship. The Bible teaches that we are to offer our bodies as living sacrifices, holy and pleasing to God, which is our spiritual act of worship.

When we worship God, we recognize his greatness and goodness, and we offer him our praise and adoration. Worship is not just something that we do on Sunday mornings but is a way of life that flows from a heart that is surrendered to God.

Zoe life is a life that is characterized by love, obedience, faithfulness, perseverance, and worship. May we all seek to live a life that is pleasing to God, as we embrace the abundant and eternal life that he has promised to us through Jesus Christ.

The Scriptures teach us that we should align our lives to the will of God. This is because God has a plan and a purpose for our lives, and when we align ourselves with his will, we experience the fullness of life that he has promised us.

Aligning our lives to the will of God requires us to surrender our will and our desires to him. This means that we must be willing to let go of our own plans and ambitions and submit ourselves to his plans and purposes for our lives.

The Bible teaches that God's will for us is good, pleasing, and perfect. When we align ourselves with his will, we experience his goodness and mercy, and we find joy and peace in knowing that we are fulfilling the purpose for which we were created.

Moreover, aligning our lives to the will of God requires us to seek him with all our hearts. This means that we must make time for prayer, study of the Scriptures, and fellowship with other believers, so that we can hear his voice and discern his will for our lives.

The Bible also teaches that aligning our lives to the will of God requires us to live a life of obedience. Jesus said, "If you love me, you will keep my commandments."

When we obey God's commands, we demonstrate our love for him and our trust in his wisdom and goodness. Obedience is not always easy, but it is necessary if we are to experience the fullness of life that God has promised us.

Furthermore, aligning our lives to the will of God requires us to live a life of faith. The Bible teaches that without faith, it is impossible to please God. Faith requires us to trust in God's promises and to believe that he is working all things together for our good. It requires us to step out in obedience even when we cannot see the outcome, knowing that God is faithful and will never leave us or forsake us.

Aligning our lives to the will of God is not always easy, but it is necessary if we are to experience the fullness of life that he has promised us. It requires us to surrender our will and our desires to him, to seek him with all our hearts, to live a life of obedience, and to walk by faith. May we all seek to align our lives to the will of God and experience the abundant life that he has promised us.

## Song of Protection

The miracle of the Red Sea is one of the most famous and awe-inspiring stories in the Bible. It tells the story of how God miraculously parted the Red Sea to allow the Israelites to cross safely on dry land, while simultaneously destroying the pursuing Egyptian army.

The story begins with the Israelites, who were being held in slavery in Egypt, being led out of Egypt by Moses after God sent plagues to persuade the Pharaoh to release them. As they journeyed towards the Promised Land, they found themselves trapped between the Red Sea and the pursuing Egyptian army.

In Exodus 14:21-22, it is written: "Then Moses stretched out his hand over the sea, and all that night the Lord drove the sea back with a strong east wind and turned it into dry land. The waters were divided, and the Israelites went through the sea on dry ground, with a wall of water on their right and on their left."

As the Israelites made their way across the sea, the Egyptians followed them, but as soon as the last Israelite had crossed, the waters rushed back in, drowning the entire Egyptian army.

This miraculous event was a powerful demonstration of God's power and protection over his people. It showed that he was able to intervene in the natural order of things and perform incredible miracles for his faithful followers.

The story of the Red Sea also teaches us the importance of faith and trust in God. When the

Israelites were trapped and facing certain doom, they turned to God and put their trust in him to save them. And God did not disappoint them. Moreover, the story has inspired countless songs, films, and works of art throughout the centuries, and continues to be a source of inspiration and wonder for people of all ages and backgrounds.

The miracle of the Red Sea is a remarkable story of God's love, power, and protection over his people. It is a testament to the importance of faith and trust in God, and a powerful reminder that even in the most desperate of situations, God is always with us, and is able to perform miracles beyond our wildest imagination.

The miracle of the Red Sea is not just a story of God's power and protection, but also a story of deliverance and freedom. The Israelites were enslaved in Egypt for hundreds of years, and their journey to the Promised Land was a journey towards liberation and a new beginning. The parting of the Red Sea represented the crossing of a threshold from slavery to freedom, and it marked the beginning of a new chapter in the history of God's people.

The Red Sea miracle also has important symbolic significance. The sea is often seen as a symbol of chaos and destruction, and the Israelites' crossing of the sea can be interpreted as a triumph over chaos and a new order being established. Moreover, the waters that destroyed the Egyptian army can be seen as a metaphor for the waters of baptism, which wash away sin and bring new life.

The story of the Red Sea has also been interpreted as a prefiguration of the baptism of Christ, which is a central sacrament in the Christian faith. Just as the Israelites were saved from destruction by passing through the waters of the Red Sea, so too are Christians saved from sin and death through the waters of baptism.

The story of the Red Sea is not just a story from the past, but also a story for the present and the future. It reminds us that God is always present with us, guiding us and protecting us through the challenges and trials of life. It also challenges us to put our faith and trust in God, even when things seem impossible or hopeless.

The miracle of the Red Sea is a powerful and inspiring story that has captured the imagination of people for thousands of years. It is a story of deliverance, freedom, and new beginnings, and it has important symbolic significance for both Jews and Christians. Ultimately, it is a story of God's love and power, and a reminder that with God, all things are possible.

The Song of Miriam is a beautiful and powerful hymn of praise found in the Bible, which was sung by Miriam, the sister of Moses, after the miraculous crossing of the Red Sea by the Israelites. The song is a celebration of God's power and faithfulness, and it has inspired countless generations of believers to lift up their voices in worship and praise.

The Song of Miriam is found in Exodus 15:1-21, and it begins with the words, "I will sing to the Lord, for he is highly exalted. The horse and its rider he has hurled into the sea." The song goes on to describe how God has delivered his people from the hand of their enemies, and how he has shown his strength and glory in the midst of their trials.

The song is a powerful expression of the joy and gratitude that the Israelites felt after their miraculous deliverance from the Egyptians. It is a celebration of God's power and faithfulness, and it shows how the Israelites recognized that their victory was not due to their own strength or prowess, but rather to the hand of God working on their behalf.

The Song of Miriam has also been interpreted as a prophetic vision of the ultimate victory of God's people over all their enemies, including sin and death. The language of the song is rich in imagery, and it evokes a sense of awe and wonder at the majesty and power of God.

The song has inspired countless works of art, music, and literature throughout the centuries, and it continues to be a source of inspiration and comfort for people of all ages and backgrounds. Its message of hope and victory in the face of adversity is as relevant today as it was in ancient times, and it serves as a reminder that God is always with us, even in the midst of our greatest challenges and trials.

The Song of Miriam is a beautiful and powerful expression of faith and worship. It celebrates God's power and faithfulness, and it reminds us that no matter what challenges we may face in life, we can always turn to God for strength and comfort. As we lift up our voices in praise and thanksgiving, we join with Miriam and all the saints who have gone before us in giving glory to God, who is worthy of all our worship and adoration.

The Song of Miriam is a testament to the power of music and singing as a means of expressing our faith and emotions. Miriam and the women of Israel lifted up their voices in song and dance, and their joy and gratitude overflowed as they praised God for his deliverance.

Music has always played an important role in worship and religious expression, and the Song of Miriam is a perfect example of this. The song has inspired countless hymns, psalms, and other musical compositions throughout the ages, and it continues to be sung and celebrated in various traditions to this day.

Moreover, the Song of Miriam is a celebration of community and shared experience. Miriam and the women of Israel sang and danced together, and their song was a collective expression of their faith and gratitude. This sense of community and shared experience is an important aspect of worship, and it reminds us that we are not alone in our faith, but rather part of a larger body of believers.

The Song of Miriam is also a reminder that God's deliverance is not just for the Israelites of old, but for all people who trust in him. The language of the song is universal, and it speaks of God's power and faithfulness in a way that transcends time and culture.

In this sense, the Song of Miriam is a song of hope and encouragement for all who face adversity and struggle in their lives. It reminds us that God is with us always, and that he is able to deliver us from even the most difficult circumstances.

The Song of Miriam is a beautiful and inspiring hymn of praise and thanksgiving. It celebrates God's power and faithfulness, and it reminds us of the importance of music, community, and shared experience in worship. As we sing and dance with Miriam and the women of Israel, we join in their joy and gratitude, and we give glory to God, who is worthy of all our worship and adoration.

The Song of Miriam, or Shirat Hayam in Hebrew, is a beautiful and poetic expression of faith and worship that appears in the Bible in Exodus 15:1-21. The Hebrew language in which it was written is rich in imagery and metaphor, and the song is structured in a way that emphasizes the repetition of certain phrases and ideas.

For example, the first line of the song, "Ashira la-Adonai ki-gaoh ga-ah" (I will sing to the Lord, for he is highly exalted), is repeated throughout the song, underscoring the central theme of worship and praise.

The Hebrew language also conveys a sense of movement and action, as the song describes God's deliverance of his people from the hand of their enemies. Phrases such as "Yam suf na'aseh hayah" (The sea was turned into dry land) and "Oz yeminekha Adonai" (Your right hand, O Lord, is majestic in power) evoke a sense of movement and drama, highlighting the miraculous nature of the Israelites' deliverance.

In addition, the Song of Miriam contains several vivid and poetic images that capture the imagination, such as the description of the sea as "ne'iravu mayim" (the waters piled up like walls) and the image of the pursuing Egyptians as "tis'akhekhu alehem ru'akh khe'ash" (the wind blew and covered them with its breath).

Overall, the Hebrew language of the Song of Miriam is a testament to the power of language and poetry in expressing our deepest emotions and beliefs. As we sing and recite this ancient hymn, we are transported back to the time of the Exodus, and we join with Miriam and the women of Israel in giving praise and thanks to God for his deliverance and faithfulness.

The Song of Miriam is not just a hymn of praise and thanksgiving, but also a declaration of faith in God's power and faithfulness. The repetition of phrases such as "Mi chamocha ba'elim Adonai" (Who is like you, O Lord, among the gods?) and "Adonai yimlokh le'olam va'ed" (The Lord will reign forever and ever) serve as a reminder of God's supremacy over all other powers and his eternal reign over the universe.

Moreover, the Song of Miriam is a celebration of the unity and solidarity of God's people. The song was sung by Miriam and the women of Israel, and it expresses the joy and gratitude of the entire community for God's deliverance. The use of the plural form throughout the song ("We will sing", "They sank like lead", etc.) emphasizes the collective nature of the Israelites' experience and underscores the importance of community and shared faith.

The Song of Miriam also has important theological implications. It shows that God is not just a distant, abstract deity, but a personal God who intervenes in human affairs to deliver his people. The song celebrates God's presence and involvement in the lives of his people, and it serves as a reminder that God is always with us, even in the most difficult and challenging circumstances.

In addition, the Song of Miriam has inspired countless works of art, music, and literature throughout the centuries, and it continues to be a source of inspiration and comfort for people of all faiths and cultures. The beauty and power of the Hebrew language, combined with the timeless themes of faith, community, and deliverance, have made the Song of Miriam one of the most beloved and enduring hymns of all time.

The Song of Miriam is a testament to the power of language, poetry, and music in expressing our deepest emotions and beliefs. It is a hymn of praise and thanksgiving, a declaration of faith in God's power and faithfulness, and a celebration of the unity and solidarity of God's people. As we sing and recite this ancient hymn, we join with Miriam and the women of Israel in giving glory to God, who is worthy of all our worship and adoration.

The story of the Israelites' crossing of the Red Sea is a powerful demonstration of the hand of God at work. The Israelites were trapped between the sea and the pursuing Egyptian army, with no apparent way of escape. But then, through the intervention of God, the sea was parted, and the Israelites were able to cross over on dry land, while the Egyptian army was destroyed by the returning waters.

The hand of God was clearly at work in this miraculous event. As the Israelites stood on the shore of the sea, with their enemies closing in on them, Moses raised his staff and called out to God for help. And God responded by sending a strong east wind that drove the waters back, creating a path of dry land for the Israelites to cross.

But the hand of God did not stop there. As the Israelites made their way across the sea, the Egyptians pursued them, but God caused their chariots to become stuck in the mud, preventing them from overtaking the Israelites. And when the last Israelite had crossed over, God caused the waters to rush back in, drowning the entire Egyptian army.

The hand of God in this miraculous event was a powerful reminder of God's love and protection for his people. It showed that God was able to intervene in the natural order of things and perform incredible miracles for his faithful followers. It also demonstrated that God was more powerful than any earthly enemy, and that he was able to deliver his people from even the most dire of circumstances.

The story of the Red Sea also teaches us important lessons about faith and trust in God. When the Israelites were trapped and facing certain doom, they turned to God and put their trust in him to save them. And God did not disappoint them. Their faith and trust in God were rewarded with a miraculous deliverance that has inspired countless generations of believers throughout history.

The hand of God was clearly at work in the miraculous crossing of the Red Sea by the Israelites. It was a powerful demonstration of God's love and protection for his people, and a reminder that with God, all things are possible. As we face our own challenges and trials in life, we can take comfort in the knowledge that God is always with us, and that he is able to perform miracles beyond our wildest imagination.

## Contributing to the Plan

The Bible is a fascinating book that contains powerful teachings on various aspects of life, including our relationship with God. One of the core teachings of the Bible is the importance of doing our part in our relationship with God. The Forcefield is enacted most through covenantal relationship.

In the Bible, we are called to actively pursue a relationship with God by obeying His commandments, seeking Him in prayer, and studying His Word. We are not passive recipients of God's grace but are called to play an active role in our spiritual growth.

One of the key ways to do our part in our relationship with God is by living a life of obedience. The Bible teaches that obedience is better than sacrifice and that our obedience to God is a reflection of our love for Him. When we choose to obey God's commands, we demonstrate our trust in Him and our willingness to follow His will for our lives.

Another important aspect of doing our part in our relationship with God is prayer. Prayer is a powerful tool that allows us to communicate with God and seek His guidance, wisdom, and strength. Through prayer, we can express our gratitude for God's blessings, confess our sins, and ask for His help in all areas of our lives.

Studying God's Word is an essential part of doing our part in our relationship with Him. The Bible is filled with wisdom, guidance, and inspiration that can help us navigate life's challenges and grow in our faith. By reading and studying the Bible, we can gain a deeper understanding of God's character, His plan for our lives, and His love for us.

The Bible teaches us that we have an active role to play in our relationship with God. By living a life of obedience, prayer, and studying His Word, we can grow closer to God and experience the fullness of His love and grace in our lives.

One of the central themes in the Bible is the idea of a covenant relationship between God and His people. A covenant is a binding agreement between two parties, and in the Bible, God establishes a covenant relationship with His people based on His love, faithfulness, and promise to bless and protect them.

However, this covenant relationship is not one-sided. God expects His people to do their part by obeying His commands and living according to His will. In Deuteronomy 6:5, God commands His people to "Love the Lord your God with all your heart and with all your soul and with all your strength." This commandment is an invitation to a deep, personal relationship with God that requires our full devotion and commitment.

Living a life of obedience to God's commands is a tangible expression of our love for Him. Jesus says in John 14:15, "If you love me, you will keep my commandments." When we choose to obey God's commands, we show Him that we trust His wisdom and His plan for our lives. Our obedience also has practical benefits for us, as we experience the peace, joy, and fulfillment that comes from living according to God's design.

Prayer is another crucial aspect of our relationship with God. In Matthew 6:6, Jesus teaches us to pray in secret, away from the distractions and pressures of the world. This intimate, personal time of prayer allows us to connect with God and seek His guidance, wisdom, and strength. Prayer is also a way for us to express our gratitude for God's blessings, confess our sins, and ask for His help in all areas of our lives.

Studying God's Word is essential for our spiritual growth and development. The Bible is the inspired Word of God, and it contains the wisdom, guidance, and inspiration that we need to navigate life's challenges and grow in our faith. In 2 Timothy 3:16-17, we read that "All Scripture is breathed out by God and profitable for teaching, for reproof, for correction, and for training in righteousness, that the man of God may be complete, equipped for every good work." When we study God's Word, we gain a deeper understanding of His character, His plan for our lives, and His love for us.

The Bible teaches us that our relationship with God is not passive, but active. By living a life of obedience, prayer, and studying His Word, we can grow closer to God and experience the fullness of His love and grace in our lives. God's invitation to a covenant relationship with Him is an incredible opportunity for us to experience His goodness and love in our lives.

One of the most important aspects of our relationship with God is obedience to His commands. In Deuteronomy 11:1, we read: "Therefore, you shall love the Lord your God, and keep His charge, His statutes, His judgments, and His commandments always." The Hebrew word for "keep" in this verse is "shamar," which means to guard, protect, and observe. This word implies a sense of responsibility and diligence in obeying God's commands, rather than a passive or superficial obedience.

In the New Testament, Jesus emphasizes the importance of obedience to God's commands. In John 14:15, Jesus says: "If you love me, keep my commandments." The Greek word for "keep" in this verse is "tereo," which means to observe, guard, and preserve. This word also implies a sense of responsibility and diligence in obeying God's commands, rather than a mere compliance.

Another important aspect of our relationship with God is prayer. In Matthew 6:6, Jesus teaches us: "But when you pray, go into your room, close the door and pray to your Father, who is unseen. Then your Father, who sees what is done in secret, will reward you." The Greek word for "room" in this verse is "tameion," which means a private or secret chamber. This word implies a sense of intimacy and privacy in our prayer life, rather than a public or showy display of prayer.

Studying God's Word is also essential for our spiritual growth and development. In 2 Timothy 3:16-17, we read: "All Scripture is God-breathed and is useful for teaching, rebuking, correcting and training in righteousness, so that the servant of God may be thoroughly equipped for every good work." The Greek word for "useful" in this verse is "ophelimos," which means profitable, advantageous, and beneficial. This word implies that studying God's Word has practical benefits for our lives, such as wisdom, guidance, and spiritual growth.

The Bible teaches us that our relationship with God requires an active and obedient response on our part. By obeying His commands, praying in intimacy and privacy, and studying His Word, we can grow closer to God and experience His blessings and rewards in our lives. The original Hebrew and Greek words used in the Bible convey a sense of responsibility, diligence, intimacy, and practical benefits, which deepen our understanding of God's invitation to a covenant relationship with Him.

One of the key aspects of our relationship with God is living a life of righteousness. In Matthew 5:20, Jesus says: "For I tell you, unless your righteousness exceeds that of the scribes and Pharisees, you will never enter the kingdom of heaven." The Greek word for "righteousness" in this verse is "dikaiosune," which means moral uprightness, justice, and conformity to God's standards. This word implies that our relationship with God requires a genuine and consistent commitment to living according to

His will, rather than a superficial or legalistic approach.

Another important aspect of our relationship with God is trust and faith. In Proverbs 3:5-6, we read: "Trust in the Lord with all your heart and lean not on your own understanding; in all your ways submit to him, and he will make your paths straight." The Hebrew word for "trust" in this verse is "batach," which means to have confidence, security, and hope in God. This word implies that our relationship with God requires a deep and unwavering trust in His goodness, faithfulness, and sovereignty, even when we don't understand His ways.

Prayer is also a crucial aspect of our relationship with God. In Philippians 4:6-7, we read: "Do not be anxious about anything, but in every situation, by prayer and petition, with thanksgiving, present your requests to God. And the peace of God, which transcends all understanding, will guard your hearts and your minds in Christ Jesus." The Greek word for "prayer" in this verse is "proseuche," which means a personal and earnest communication with God. This word implies that our relationship with God requires a genuine and intimate prayer life, rather than a formal or ritualistic approach.

Studying God's Word is also essential for our relationship with God. In Psalm 119:105, we read: "Your word is a lamp for my feet, a light on my path." The Hebrew word for "word" in this verse is "dabar," which means a spoken or written message from God. This word implies that studying God's Word is essential for receiving guidance, wisdom, and revelation from God.

The Bible teaches us that our relationship with God requires a deep and genuine commitment to righteousness, trust, prayer, and studying His Word. By living according to His will, trusting in His goodness and sovereignty, communicating with Him in intimacy and earnestness, and studying His Word for guidance and wisdom, we can experience the fullness of His love, grace, and blessings in our lives.

One of the most important aspects of our relationship with God is love. In Mark 12:30-31, Jesus teaches us: "Love the Lord your God with all your heart and with all your soul and with all your mind and with all your strength. The second is this: Love your neighbor as yourself. There is no commandment greater than these." The Greek word for "love" in this verse is "agape," which means a selfless, sacrificial, and unconditional love. This word implies that our relationship with God requires a genuine and sacrificial love for Him, as well as a love for others that reflects His character and will.

Another important aspect of our relationship with God is humility. In James 4:6, we read: "But he gives us more grace. That is why Scripture says: 'God opposes the proud but shows favor to the humble.'" The Greek word for "opposes" in this verse is "antitassomai," which means to resist, oppose, or set oneself against. This word implies that our relationship with God requires a humble and submissive attitude, rather than a proud or self-centered one.

Prayer is also an essential aspect of our relationship with God. In Ephesians 6:18, we read: "And pray in the Spirit on all occasions with all kinds of prayers and requests. With this in mind, be alert and always keep on praying for all the Lord's people." The Greek word for "prayer" in this verse is "proseuche," which means a personal and earnest communication with God. This word implies that our relationship with God requires a consistent and persistent prayer life, as well as a sensitivity to His will and purposes.

Studying God's Word is another crucial aspect of our relationship with God. In 2 Timothy 2:15, we read: "Do your best to present yourself to God as one approved, a worker who does not need to be ashamed and who correctly handles the word of truth." The Greek word for "correctly handle" in this verse is "orthotomeo," which means to cut straight, divide rightly, or handle accurately. This word implies that studying God's Word requires a diligent and careful approach, as well as a willingness to apply its truths to our lives.

The Bible teaches us that our relationship with God requires a genuine and sacrificial love for Him and others, a humble and submissive attitude, a consistent and persistent prayer life, and a diligent and careful study of His Word. By living according to His will, trusting in His goodness and sovereignty, communicating with Him in intimacy and earnestness, and studying His Word for guidance and wisdom, we can experience the fullness of His love, grace, and blessings in our lives.

The idea that faith without works is dead is a powerful teaching found in the Bible, and it has significant implications for our relationship with God and our daily lives.

In James 2:14-17, we read: "What good is it, my brothers and sisters, if someone claims to have faith but has no deeds? Can such faith save them? Suppose a brother or a sister is without clothes and daily food. If one of you says to them, 'Go in peace; keep warm and well fed,' but does nothing about their physical needs, what good is it? In the same way, faith by itself, if it is not accompanied by action, is dead."

This passage teaches us that faith and action are inseparable, and that genuine faith produces good works. The Greek word for "dead" in this passage is "nekros," which means lifeless, inactive, and unproductive. This word implies that faith that is not accompanied by action is meaningless and ineffective.

The Bible teaches that we are saved by faith alone, but our faith should produce good works as evidence of our salvation. In Ephesians 2:8-10, we read: "For it is by grace you have been saved, through faith—and this is not from yourselves, it is the gift of God—not by works, so that no one can boast. For we are God's handiwork, created in Christ Jesus to do good works, which God prepared in advance for us to do."

Our faith in God should motivate us to live a life of love, obedience, and service. When we believe in God's love and grace, we are empowered to love and serve others with compassion and kindness. When we trust in God's wisdom and guidance, we are enabled to obey His commands and follow His will for our lives. And when we rely on God's strength and power, we are emboldened to overcome our weaknesses and limitations.

The Bible teaches us that faith without works is dead, and that genuine faith produces good works as evidence of our salvation. Our faith should motivate us to live a life of love, obedience, and service, as we trust in God's love, wisdom, and power to guide us. When we combine our faith with action, we can make a positive impact on the world and experience the fullness of God's blessings in our lives.

The idea that faith without works is dead is not just a theoretical or theological concept, but it has practical implications for our daily lives. Our faith in God should inspire us to live a life of love, compassion, and service towards others.

In Matthew 25:35-36, Jesus says: "For I was hungry and you gave me something to eat, I was thirsty and you gave me something to drink, I was a stranger and you invited me in, I needed clothes and you clothed me, I was sick and you looked after me, I was in prison and you came to visit me." This passage teaches us that our faith should move us to help those who are in need, to show kindness and hospitality to strangers, and to care for the sick and imprisoned.

James 1:27 says: "Religion that God our Father accepts as pure and faultless is this: to look after orphans and widows in their distress and to keep oneself from being polluted by the world." This verse highlights the importance of caring for the vulnerable and marginalized in society, and also emphasizes the need for personal holiness and purity.

Our faith should also motivate us to share the good news of the gospel with others. In Mark 16:15, Jesus says: "Go into all the world and preach the gospel to all creation." This verse commands us to share the message of God's love and salvation with everyone, regardless of their background or status.

The concept of faith without works being dead reminds us that our faith in God should not be passive or theoretical, but it should produce tangible and practical results in our lives. Our

115

faith should inspire us to love and serve others, to care for the vulnerable and marginalized, to live a life of holiness and purity, and to share the gospel message with others. When we combine our faith with action, we can make a positive impact on the world and bring glory to God.

# Intimacy

The Bible is filled with teachings about intimacy with God, which refers to the deep and personal relationship that we can have with our Creator. It is a relationship that goes beyond mere knowledge of God and involves a heartfelt connection that brings us closer to Him. In this post, we will explore some of the key teachings from the Bible about intimacy with God.

Intimacy with God requires a personal relationship. God desires to have a personal relationship with each one of us. In the book of Isaiah, God says, "I have called you by name; you are mine" (Isaiah 43:1). This means that

God knows us intimately, and He wants us to know Him in the same way. The Bible tells us that we can have a personal relationship with God through faith in Jesus Christ, who is the way, the truth, and the life (John 14:6).

Intimacy with God involves spending time with Him. Just like any other relationship, intimacy with God requires spending time with Him. This means setting aside time to pray, read the Bible, and worship Him. In Psalm 46:10, God says, "Be still, and know that I am God." This verse reminds us of the importance of quieting our minds and hearts so that we can hear from God and experience His presence.

Intimacy with God requires obedience. Jesus said, "If you love me, keep my commands" (John 14:15). Obedience to God's commands is an essential part of intimacy with Him. When we obey God, we show our love and respect for

Him, and we demonstrate our trust in His wisdom and goodness.

Intimacy with God involves trust. Trusting in God is an essential part of intimacy with Him. In Proverbs 3:5-6, we read, "Trust in the Lord with all your heart and lean not on your own understanding; in all your ways submit to him, and he will make your paths straight." Trusting in God means believing that He is always working for our good, even when we can't see it.

Intimacy with God brings transformation. When we spend time with God and obey His commands, we begin to experience transformation in our lives. In 2 Corinthians 3:18, we read, "And we all, who with unveiled faces contemplate the Lord's glory, are being transformed into his image with ever-increasing glory, which comes from the Lord, who is the

Spirit." As we become more intimate with God, we become more like Him, and our lives are transformed.

The Bible teaches us that intimacy with God is a personal and deep relationship that requires spending time with Him, obeying His commands, trusting in Him, and experiencing transformation in our lives. As we pursue intimacy with God, we will experience the joy and peace that comes from being in His presence, and we will become more like Him.

Intimacy with God involves vulnerability. To truly experience intimacy with God, we must be vulnerable with Him. This means opening up our hearts and sharing our deepest fears, struggles, and joys with Him. In Psalm 62:8, we read, "Trust in him at all times, you people; pour out your hearts to him, for God is our refuge." When we pour out our hearts to God, we allow Him to work in us and through us in ways we never thought possible.

Intimacy with God is a two-way conversation. Intimacy with God is not just about us talking to God, but also about Him speaking to us. God speaks to us through His Word, through other people, and through the Holy Spirit. In John 10:27, Jesus says, "My sheep listen to my voice; I know them, and they follow me." As we spend time with God and listen to His voice, we will grow in our intimacy with Him and gain a deeper understanding of His plans for our lives.

Intimacy with God is a lifelong journey. Intimacy with God is not something that happens overnight; it is a lifelong journey. It requires a daily commitment to spend time with God, seek His guidance, and obey His commands. In Philippians 3:10, the apostle Paul says, "I want to know Christ—yes, to know the power of his resurrection and participation in his sufferings, becoming like him in his death." Paul understood that intimacy with God is an ongoing process, and he was committed to growing in his relationship with Him.

Intimacy with God is available to all. Intimacy with God is not reserved for a select few; it is available to all who seek it. In Acts 10:34-35, we read, "Then Peter began to speak: 'I now realize how true it is that God does not show favoritism but accepts from every nation the one who fears him and does what is right.'" God's love and grace are available to all who seek Him, regardless of their background or circumstances.

Intimacy with God is a personal and deep relationship that involves spending time with Him, obeying His commands, trusting in Him, and experiencing transformation in our lives. It also involves vulnerability, a two-way conversation, a lifelong journey, and is available to all who seek it. As we seek to grow in our intimacy with God, we can trust that He will guide us and transform us into the people He created us to be. As we continue to explore the topic of intimacy with God, there are a few more important aspects to consider.

Intimacy with God requires surrender. Intimacy with God involves surrendering our will to His. This means letting go of our own plans and desires and trusting that God's plans for us are better. In Romans 12:1-2, we read, "Therefore, I urge you, brothers and sisters, in view of God's mercy, to offer your bodies as a living sacrifice, holy and pleasing to God—this is your true and proper worship. Do not conform to the pattern of this world, but be transformed by the renewing of your mind. Then you will be able to test and approve what God's will is—his good, pleasing and perfect will." As we surrender our lives to God, He transforms us and leads us on the path He has for us.

Intimacy with God brings healing. Intimacy with God brings healing to our brokenness. In Psalm 147:3, we read, "He heals the brokenhearted and binds up their wounds." When we bring our pain and brokenness to God, He comforts us and heals us. As we grow in our intimacy with God, we experience His love and grace in new and profound ways, and our hearts are transformed.

Intimacy with God involves community. Intimacy with God is not just a private, individual experience, but also involves community. We were created for community, and God desires for us to connect with others who share our faith. In Hebrews 10:24-25, we read, "And let us consider how we may spur one another on toward love and good deeds, not giving up meeting together, as some are in the habit of doing, but encouraging one another—and all the more as you see the Day approaching." As we connect with other believers, we encourage each other and grow together in our intimacy with God.

Intimacy with God brings joy and peace. Intimacy with God brings a deep sense of joy and peace to our lives. In John 15:11, Jesus says, "I have told you this so that my joy may be in you and that your joy may be complete." When we experience intimacy with God, we are filled with His joy and peace, which transcends our circumstances and gives us hope and strength.

Intimacy with God is a personal and deep relationship that involves surrender, healing, community, joy, and peace. As we seek to grow in our intimacy with God, we can trust that He will guide us and transform us into the people He created us to be. May we continue to pursue intimacy with God and experience the fullness of His love and grace in our lives.

The Bible speaks of God's love for us and the depth of our relationship with Him, but this is not in a sexual context. While there are poetic and metaphorical descriptions of God's love for us, these are not meant to be taken in a literal sense.

However, there are passages in the Bible that allude to the intimacy and closeness that we can experience with God. In the book of Song of Solomon, there are poetic descriptions of the love and desire between a husband and wife, which can also be interpreted as a metaphor for the love and desire between God and His people.

In Song of Solomon 4:9-10, the bridegroom says to his bride, "You have stolen my heart, my sister, my bride; you have stolen my heart with one glance of your eyes, with one jewel of your necklace. How delightful is your love, my sister, my bride! How much more pleasing is your love than wine, and the fragrance of your perfume more than any spice!"

While these verses are a metaphor for the love between a husband and wife, they also speak to the deep intimacy and closeness that we can experience with God. The love and desire described here are not sexual, but rather speak to the depth of the relationship between two people who are completely devoted to one another.

In Psalm 63:1, David speaks of his longing for God, saying, "You, God, are my God, earnestly I seek you; I thirst for you, my whole being longs for you, in a dry and parched land where there is no water." This verse speaks to the deep yearning and desire that we can have for God, a desire that goes beyond physical attraction or sexual intimacy.

While there are no explicit references in the Bible to sexual intimacy with God, there are passages that allude to the deep intimacy and closeness that we can experience with Him. The love and desire described in these passages are not sexual, but rather speak to the depth of the relationship that we can have with God. As we seek to grow in our intimacy with God, may we continue to explore and deepen the richness of our relationship with Him.

One example of this is found in the Gospel of John, where Jesus speaks of the intimate relationship that He has with His followers. In John 15:4-5, Jesus says, "Remain in me, as I also remain in you. No branch can bear fruit by itself; it must remain in the vine. Neither can you bear fruit unless you remain in me. I am the vine; you are the branches. If you remain in me and I in you, you will bear much fruit; apart from me you can do nothing."

The Greek word used for "remain" in this passage is "meno," which means to abide, stay, or continue in. This word emphasizes the deep and ongoing nature of the relationship that Jesus desires to have with His followers. It is not a casual or superficial relationship, but one that requires a continuous commitment to abide in Christ.

Another example of the depth of intimacy that we can have with God is found in the book of Romans. In Romans 8:38-39, Paul speaks of the inseparable love that we have in Christ, saying, "For I am convinced that neither death nor life, neither angels nor demons, neither the present nor the future, nor any powers, neither height nor depth, nor anything else in all creation, will be able to separate us from the love of God that is in Christ Jesus our Lord."

The Greek word used for "love" in this passage is "agape," which is a selfless, sacrificial love that seeks the highest good of the other person. This type of love emphasizes the depth of God's love for us and the unbreakable nature of our relationship with Him.

While there are no references in the New Testament that suggest sexual intimacy with God, there are passages that speak to the deep intimacy and closeness that we can experience with Him. The Greek language used in these passages emphasizes the depth and ongoing nature of the relationship that we can have with God, as well as the selfless love that He has for us. As we seek to grow in our intimacy with God, may we continue to abide in Him and experience the richness of His love and grace.

Building on the previous points, it is important to note that the Greek language used in the New Testament highlights the relational nature of our connection with God. The Greek word for "relationship" is "koinonia," which is often translated as "fellowship" or "communion." This word emphasizes the idea of a shared life, where we are united with God and with one another in a deep and meaningful way.

In 1 Corinthians 1:9, Paul speaks of this shared life, saying, "God is faithful, who has called you into fellowship (koinonia) with his Son, Jesus Christ our Lord." This verse emphasizes the idea that we are not only called into a relationship with God, but also into a community of believers who share in that relationship.

The Greek word for "unity" is "henotes," which emphasizes the idea of oneness and harmony. In John 17:20-23, Jesus prays for unity among His followers, saying, "My prayer is not for them alone. I pray also for those who will believe in me through their message, that all of them may be one, Father, just as you are in me and I am in you. May they also be in us so that the world may believe that you have sent me. I have given them the glory that you gave me, that they may be one as we are one— I in them and you in me—so that they may be brought to complete unity. Then the world will know that you sent me and have loved them even as you have loved me."

This passage emphasizes the depth of intimacy that we can have with God and with one another, as we share in the same life and purpose. It also emphasizes the importance of unity among believers, as a way of bearing witness to the love and grace of God to the world.

The New Testament Greek language emphasizes the relational nature of our connection with God, highlighting the depth of intimacy and shared life that we can experience with Him and with one another. As we seek to grow in our intimacy with God, may we also seek to build unity and fellowship with our fellow believers, as a way of bearing witness to the love and grace of God to the world.

Expanding on the theme of relational intimacy with God in the New Testament Greek language, it is important to note that the concept of love is central to this relationship. The Greek language has multiple words for love, including

133

"philia" (friendship love), "eros" (romantic love), and "agape" (selfless, sacrificial love).

It is the latter type of love, agape, that is most often used in the New Testament to describe God's love for us and our love for Him. In John 3:16, we read, "For God so loved (agape) the world that he gave his one and only Son, that whoever believes in him shall not perish but have eternal life." This verse emphasizes the selfless, sacrificial nature of God's love for us, which is demonstrated through the gift of His Son, Jesus Christ.

Similarly, in 1 John 4:8-10, we read, "Whoever does not love (agape) does not know God, because God is love. This is how God showed his love among us: He sent his one and only Son into the world that we might live through him. This is love: not that we loved God, but that he loved us and sent his Son as an atoning sacrifice for our sins." Again, this passage emphasizes the selfless, sacrificial nature of God's love for us, and the importance of responding to that love with our own love for Him and for one another.

The Greek word for "know" is "ginosko," which emphasizes a deep and experiential knowledge of God. In John 17:3, Jesus says, "Now this is eternal life: that they know (ginosko) you, the only true God, and Jesus Christ, whom you have sent." This verse emphasizes the importance of a deep and personal relationship with God, one that goes beyond mere intellectual knowledge or belief.

The New Testament Greek language emphasizes the relational nature of our connection with God, highlighting the importance of a deep and personal relationship with Him based on selfless, sacrificial love. As we seek to grow in our intimacy with God, may we also seek to demonstrate that love to one another, building unity and fellowship in the body of Christ.

Closeness with God is a beautiful and transformative experience that brings us into a deeper relationship with Him. It is a journey of growing intimacy with God, where we learn to trust Him more fully, seek Him more passionately, and love Him more deeply.

The Bible tells us that God desires intimacy with us. In James 4:8, we read, "Come near to God and he will come near to you." This verse emphasizes the importance of taking the initiative to draw near to God, which He will reciprocate with His own presence and closeness.

One way to cultivate closeness with God is through prayer. Prayer is not just a way of making requests to God, but also a way of building our relationship with Him. Through prayer, we open our hearts to God and allow Him to work in us and through us. In Philippians 4:6-7, we read, "Do not be anxious about anything, but in every situation, by prayer and petition, with thanksgiving, present your requests to God. And the peace of God, which transcends all understanding, will guard your hearts and your minds in Christ Jesus." This verse emphasizes the power of prayer to bring us into God's peace and presence.

Another way to cultivate closeness with God is through worship. Worship is not just a way of praising God, but also a way of experiencing His presence and power. In Psalm 100:2-4, we read, "Worship the Lord with gladness; come before him with joyful songs. Know that the Lord is God. It is he who made us, and we are his; we are his people, the sheep of his pasture.

Enter his gates with thanksgiving and his courts with praise; give thanks to him and praise his name." This verse emphasizes the importance of worship as a way of entering into God's presence and experiencing His goodness.

Finally, cultivating closeness with God involves an ongoing commitment to obey Him and follow His ways. In John 14:15, Jesus says, "If you love me, keep my commands." This verse emphasizes the importance of obedience as a way of demonstrating our love for God and growing in our relationship with Him.

Cultivating closeness with God is a journey of growing intimacy with Him through prayer, worship, and obedience. As we seek to draw near to God, we can trust that He will draw near to us, bringing us into a deeper and more transformative relationship with Him. May we continue to pursue closeness with God with passion and persistence, knowing that He desires to be close to us more than we could ever imagine.

God in All Things

God is in all things. And not only is God in all things, but all things are working together for your good – and for your protection. I wanted to include this chapter as a way to say that in all of life, the hand of God is at work. It's time to begin to see the God of "All Things."

All things work together in life for the good of those who love God. This idea comes from a verse in the Christian Bible, specifically in Romans 8:28, which says, "And we know that all things work together for good to them that love God, to them who are the called according to his purpose."

This verse implies that everything that happens in life, both good and bad, can be used for a greater purpose for those who love God. It acknowledges that life can be difficult and challenging, but encourages people to have faith that everything happens for a reason and that God has a plan for their lives. This concept can be comforting for those who have faith, as it provides hope and assurance that even in difficult times, they are not alone and that there is a greater purpose to their struggles.

However, it's important to note that this belief should not be used to dismiss or diminish the struggles and suffering of others, as everyone's experiences are valid and important. It's also important to recognize that not everyone shares this belief and that there are different interpretations and understandings of this verse. Whether one believes in this concept or not, it highlights the importance of finding purpose and meaning in life, even in the face of adversity. It encourages individuals to seek out something greater than themselves and to have faith in a higher power or purpose.

The idea that all things work together in life for the good of those who love God can be a source of comfort and hope for those who have faith. It emphasizes the importance of finding purpose and meaning in life, even in difficult times. However, it's important to approach this belief with empathy and respect for others' experiences and beliefs.

Romans 8:28 is a verse from the Christian Bible that is often quoted and used as a source of comfort for believers. It reads, "And we know that all things work together for good to them that love God, to them who are the called according to his purpose."

This verse is part of a larger passage in the book of Romans, written by the apostle Paul, in which he explores the concept of salvation and the role of the Holy Spirit in the life of a believer. In this particular verse, Paul is reminding the Romans that everything that happens in their lives, whether good or bad, can be used for a greater purpose if they love God and are called according to His purpose.

The concept of "all things working together for good" does not mean that everything that happens in a believer's life will be good or pleasant. Instead, it suggests that even in the face of difficult circumstances or suffering, God is still working behind the scenes to bring about a greater good. This can include things like personal growth, increased faith, or the opportunity to help others who may be going through similar struggles.

It's important to note that the verse does not suggest that all things are good in and of themselves, or that suffering is something that should be desired or sought after. Instead, it emphasizes the idea that even in the midst of difficult circumstances, God can use those experiences to bring about a greater good in the life of a believer.

Overall, Romans 8:28 is a powerful reminder for Christians that even in the midst of life's challenges and struggles, they can find hope and comfort in the knowledge that God is working all things together for their good. Romans 8:28 is a verse that has been a source of comfort and encouragement for Christians for centuries. It speaks to the idea that, for those who love God and are called according to His purpose, there is a higher plan at work in their lives. This verse can provide a sense of peace and hope in times of difficulty, as it assures believers that God is in control and is working to bring about a greater good.

However, it's important to note that this verse does not promise an easy life or that everything will always go according to plan. Instead, it suggests that even in the face of adversity and suffering, God can use those experiences to bring about something positive. This can include personal growth, increased faith, and opportunities to help others who may be going through similar struggles.

One of the key aspects of this verse is the idea of being called according to His purpose. This suggests that there is a specific plan for each believer's life and that everything that happens is part of that plan. For those who have faith, this can provide a sense of purpose and meaning in their lives, as they seek to understand what God's plan is for them.

It's important to note that the idea of "all things working together for good" is not unique to Christianity. Many religions and belief systems have similar concepts, which speak to the idea that there is a higher purpose to our experiences and that suffering can be transformative.

Overall, Romans 8:28 is a powerful reminder for believers that even in the midst of life's challenges and struggles, there is hope and purpose to be found. It encourages them to trust in God's plan and to seek out opportunities to grow and serve others, even in difficult circumstances.

Romans 8:28 is not just a comforting verse for believers, but also a challenging one. It calls believers to trust in God's plan, even when things seem to be going wrong or when they are facing difficult situations. It reminds them that

God is in control and is able to work all things together for good.

However, this verse can also be misunderstood or misinterpreted. Some people may believe that it means that everything that happens in their lives is God's will, or that they should passively accept suffering without seeking to change their circumstances. But this is not what the verse is saying. Instead, it emphasizes the idea that even in difficult circumstances, believers can actively seek to grow, learn, and serve others, trusting that God is working in their lives for a greater purpose.

The concept of "all things working together for good" can be difficult to understand or accept, especially in the face of tragedy or suffering. However, for believers, it provides a source of hope and comfort, reminding them that there is a higher purpose to their experiences and that God is with them every step of the way.

Ultimately, Romans 8:28 speaks to the idea that life is not always easy, but that there is a greater purpose to our experiences. It calls believers to trust in God's plan, even when things are difficult, and to seek out opportunities to grow and serve others. In doing so, they can find hope, peace, and purpose in the midst of life's challenges.

Romans 8:28 is a well-known verse in the Christian Bible, and it can be useful to explore its original Greek language to gain a deeper understanding of its meaning.

The Greek word translated as "all things" in this verse is πᾶς (pas), which can refer to every kind or variety of thing. This includes both good and bad things, which is important to note in the context of this verse. The idea is that even the difficult or painful experiences in life can be used for a greater purpose.

The phrase "work together" is translated from the Greek word συνεργέω (synergeó), which means to work together, cooperate, or be effective. This emphasizes the idea that even seemingly disparate or unrelated events in a believer's life can be brought together for a greater purpose.

The Greek word translated as "good" in this verse is ἀγαθός (agathos), which can refer to that which is morally excellent or beneficial. This emphasizes the idea that God's plan is ultimately for the good of believers, even if it may not always seem that way in the moment.

Finally, the phrase "called according to his purpose" is translated from the Greek words κλητός (klētos) and πρόθεσις (prothesis). Klētos refers to being called, invited, or chosen, while prothesis refers to a plan or intention. This suggests that believers who are called by God have a specific purpose or plan for their lives, and that all things work together to bring about that plan.

Exploring the original Greek language of Romans 8:28 can provide a deeper understanding of its meaning. It emphasizes the idea that all things, both good and bad, can be used for a greater purpose in the lives of believers who are called according to God's plan. The verse encourages believers to trust in God's ultimate goodness and to seek opportunities for growth and service, even in the midst of difficult circumstances.

God is working, even when it seems otherwise. Many people find comfort in the belief that everything in life happens for a reason, and that even the most difficult or trying experiences can ultimately lead to growth and positive outcomes. This is a common theme in many religious and spiritual traditions, including Christianity.

One biblical example of this is the story of Joseph in the book of Genesis. Joseph was one of twelve sons of Jacob and was favored by his father. This led to jealousy among his brothers, who sold him into slavery and told their father that he had been killed by wild animals.

Joseph was taken to Egypt and sold into the household of Potiphar, an Egyptian official. However, when Potiphar's wife accused Joseph of attempting to seduce her, he was thrown into prison. Despite these difficult circumstances, Joseph maintained his faith in God and eventually rose to a position of power in Egypt, second only to Pharaoh himself.

Through a series of events, Joseph was able to reconcile with his brothers and help them during a time of famine. In the end, Joseph recognized that God had used his difficult experiences to bring about a greater good, both for him personally and for his family and the people of Egypt.

This story highlights the idea that even when things seem to be going wrong, people can trust that God is working behind the scenes to bring about positive outcomes. It also emphasizes the importance of maintaining faith and trust in God, even in the face of difficult circumstances.

Overall, the story of Joseph serves as a powerful reminder that even the most challenging experiences in life can ultimately lead to positive outcomes if people maintain their faith and trust in something greater than themselves. It encourages people to seek out opportunities

153

for growth and to trust that God is always working for their good, even when things seem to be going wrong.

The story of Joseph is a powerful example of how God can work all things together for good, even in the midst of difficult circumstances. It reminds us that God's plans are often greater than our own, and that our struggles can be used to bring about positive outcomes that we may not have anticipated.

One of the key lessons from the story of Joseph is the importance of faith and trust in God. Despite the many setbacks and challenges he faced, Joseph never lost faith that God was with him and working for his good. He was able to maintain his trust in God even when his circumstances seemed dire, and this ultimately led to his eventual success and reconciliation with his family.

This story also highlights the importance of perseverance and resilience in the face of adversity. Joseph faced many obstacles, from being sold into slavery by his own brothers to being falsely accused of a crime he didn't commit. However, he never gave up, and he continued to trust that God was with him, even in his darkest moments.

The story of Joseph is just one example of how God can work all things together for good. Many other biblical stories and personal testimonies demonstrate this same idea. It is a powerful reminder that no matter what we may be going through, we can always find hope and comfort in the knowledge that God is working for our good.

Ultimately, the story of Joseph is a testament to the power of faith, resilience, and perseverance in the face of adversity. It shows us that even the most challenging circumstances can be used to bring about positive outcomes, and that God's plans are often greater than our own. It encourages us to trust in God's goodness and to seek out opportunities for growth and positive change, even in the midst of difficult times.

I think of a dear friend of the ministry named David who had a successful business, a loving family, and a comfortable life. However, one day, everything changed when he was diagnosed with a serious illness.

David was devastated. He had always been a healthy and active person, and he couldn't believe that something like this could happen to him. He had to undergo extensive treatments and surgeries, and the process was long and painful.

During this difficult time, David began to question his faith. He couldn't understand why

God would allow something so terrible to happen to him, and he felt angry and resentful. He struggled to find meaning and purpose in his life, and he felt hopeless and lost.

However, as David continued his treatment and recovery, something miraculous began to happen. He started to meet other patients who were also struggling with serious illnesses, and he began to see how his own experience could be used to help others.

David started volunteering at a local hospital, where he would visit patients and share his story of hope and healing. He started a support group for people who were going through similar struggles, and he became a source of comfort and inspiration for those who needed it most.

Through this experience, David realized that God had turned something bad into something good. He saw that his illness had given him a new purpose in life, and that he was able to help others in ways he never could have imagined.

David's faith was restored, and he felt a sense of peace and joy that he had never felt before. He realized that God had been with him all along, even in the midst of his struggles, and that He had a greater plan for his life.

In the end, David was cured of his illness, but his experience had transformed him in ways that went far beyond his physical health. He had discovered a new sense of purpose and meaning, and he had learned to trust in God's plan, even when things seemed impossible.

David's story is a powerful example of how God can turn something bad into something good. It reminds us that even in the midst of our darkest struggles, there is always hope, and that God's plans are often greater than our own.

Positioning

The Bible is filled with teachings about God's plan and purpose for our lives. As Christians, it is essential to understand and position ourselves to align with God's plan and purpose for our lives. In this post, we will explore what the Bible teaches about positioning ourselves to God's plan and purpose.

Seek God's will. The Bible teaches that seeking God's will is crucial in positioning ourselves to His plan and purpose. Proverbs 3:5-6 says, "Trust in the Lord with all your heart and lean not on your understanding; in all your ways submit to him, and he will make your paths straight." Seeking God's will requires humility and a willingness to surrender our desires and plans to God.

Live a life of obedience. Living a life of obedience to God's word is another crucial aspect of positioning ourselves to His plan and purpose. In John 14:15, Jesus says, "If you love me, keep my commands." When we obey God's word, we demonstrate our love and devotion to Him. Obedience to God's word also helps us to stay on the right path and avoid straying from God's plan for our lives.

Develop a relationship with God. Developing a close relationship with God is also essential in positioning ourselves to His plan and purpose. In James 4:8, we are encouraged to "Draw near to God, and he will draw near to you." Developing a relationship with God involves spending time in prayer, reading the Bible, and worshiping Him. As we draw closer to God, He reveals His plan and purpose for our lives.

Trust in God's timing. Trusting in God's timing is another vital aspect of positioning ourselves to His plan and purpose. In Ecclesiastes 3:1, we read, "There is a time for everything, and a season for every activity under the heavens." Sometimes, we may feel impatient or frustrated with the pace of God's plan for our lives. However, trusting in God's timing and remaining patient allows us to stay focused on His plan and purpose.

Use our gifts and talents for God's glory. Using our gifts and talents for God's glory is also essential in positioning ourselves to His plan and purpose. In 1 Peter 4:10, we read, "Each of you should use whatever gift you have received to serve others, as faithful stewards of God's grace in its various forms." God has given each of us unique gifts and talents, and when we use them to serve Him, we position ourselves to fulfill His plan and purpose for our lives.

The Bible teaches us that positioning ourselves to God's plan and purpose requires seeking His will, living a life of obedience, developing a relationship with God, trusting in His timing, and using our gifts and talents for His glory. When we position ourselves to God's plan and purpose, we experience peace, joy, and fulfillment in our lives.

One of the most significant benefits of positioning ourselves to God's plan and purpose is the sense of direction and clarity that it brings to our lives. Without a clear understanding of God's plan for our lives, we can easily become lost or feel aimless, but when we seek to align ourselves with His will, we gain a sense of purpose that brings meaning and direction to our lives.

Another benefit of positioning ourselves to God's plan and purpose is that it allows us to experience the fullness of God's blessings. When we are obedient to God's word and live in alignment with His plan, we can expect to receive blessings and favor from Him. In Malachi 3:10, God promises to open the windows of heaven and pour out blessings on those who bring their tithes and offerings to Him.

Positioning ourselves to God's plan and purpose also gives us the ability to impact the world around us positively. When we live according to God's will, we become instruments of His love, grace, and mercy to those around us. As we use our gifts and talents to serve others, we become agents of change and transformation in our communities.

However, positioning ourselves to God's plan and purpose is not always easy. There may be times when we experience setbacks, disappointments, or difficulties along the way. But in these moments, we can take comfort in the promise of Romans 8:28, which says, "And we know that in all things God works for the good of those who love him, who have been called according to his purpose."

Ultimately, positioning ourselves to God's plan and purpose requires a deep commitment to following Him, even when it is difficult or inconvenient. As we seek to align ourselves with His will, we can trust that He will guide us and lead us into the life that He has planned for us.

Another important aspect of positioning ourselves to God's plan and purpose is to remain focused on Him and His word. We live in a world that is full of distractions and temptations, but when we stay focused on God and His truth, we are less likely to be swayed by the lies and deceptions of the world.

Additionally, positioning ourselves to God's plan and purpose requires a willingness to let go of our own desires and plans. This can be difficult, especially when we have a particular vision for our lives that we want to see fulfilled. However, when we surrender our plans to God and trust in His will, we open ourselves up to the abundance of blessings and opportunities that He has in store for us.

Furthermore, positioning ourselves to God's plan and purpose involves a process of continual growth and transformation. As we seek to become more like Christ, we must be willing to let go of our old ways of thinking and living and embrace the new life that He has for us. This process can be challenging at times, but with the help of the Holy Spirit, we can grow and mature in our faith.

It is important to remember that positioning ourselves to God's plan and purpose is a journey, not a destination. We will face challenges and setbacks along the way, but if we remain steadfast in our faith and committed to following God, we can be confident that He will guide us and lead us into the fullness of His plan for our lives.

Positioning ourselves to God's plan and purpose is a lifelong journey that requires faith, obedience, and a deep commitment to following Him. As we seek to align ourselves with His will, we can experience the fullness of His blessings and become agents of His love and grace to those around us.

Another critical aspect of positioning ourselves to God's plan and purpose is the importance of prayer. Prayer is our direct line of communication with God, and it allows us to bring our hopes, fears, and desires before Him. When we pray, we can ask for guidance and direction in our lives, and we can trust that God will answer our prayers according to His perfect will.

Moreover, positioning ourselves to God's plan and purpose requires a willingness to step out in faith and take risks. God often calls us to step outside of our comfort zones and do things that may seem daunting or unfamiliar to us. However, when we trust in His guidance and take these risks, we can experience tremendous growth and blessings in our lives.

Another important aspect of positioning ourselves to God's plan and purpose is the importance of community. God created us to live in community with one another, and when we surround ourselves with fellow believers who are also seeking to follow God's plan, we can encourage and support one another on the journey.

Furthermore, positioning ourselves to God's plan and purpose requires a willingness to forgive others and extend grace. We are all human and prone to making mistakes, but when we choose to forgive others and extend grace, we reflect the love and mercy of God to those around us.

Positioning ourselves to God's plan and purpose is a holistic journey that involves every aspect of our lives. It requires a deep commitment to following God, a willingness to take risks and step outside of our comfort zones, a reliance on prayer and community, and a spirit of forgiveness and grace. As we seek to align ourselves with God's plan and purpose, we can experience the fullness of His blessings and become agents of His love and grace to a world in need.

Psalm 91 is a beautiful and powerful psalm that encourages greater closeness to God. This psalm speaks of the protection and shelter that God provides for those who trust in Him. It is a psalm that gives us hope and assurance in the midst of life's uncertainties, and it reminds us of the incredible love and care that God has for us.

The psalm begins with these words: "Whoever dwells in the shelter of the Most High will rest in the shadow of the Almighty." This verse sets the tone for the rest of the psalm, reminding us that when we dwell in the shelter of God's presence, we can find rest and peace even in the midst of life's storms.

Verse 2 goes on to say, "I will say of the Lord, 'He is my refuge and my fortress, my God, in whom I trust.'" This verse encourages us to speak out our trust and confidence in God. When we declare that God is our refuge and fortress, we are reminding ourselves of His protection and strength in our lives.

As we continue through the psalm, we see numerous promises of God's care and protection. We read of His protection from deadly diseases, from the terror of the night, and from the arrows that fly by day. We are reminded that He will not let our foot slip and that He will be with us in times of trouble.

One of the most beautiful promises in the psalm comes in verses 14-16, where God Himself speaks to us: "Because he loves me," says the

Lord, "I will rescue him; I will protect him, for he acknowledges my name. He will call on me, and I will answer him; I will be with him in trouble, I will deliver him and honor him. With long life I will satisfy him and show him my salvation."

These verses remind us that when we love God and acknowledge His name, He promises to rescue and protect us. He promises to be with us in times of trouble, to answer our prayers, and to show us His salvation. As we draw closer to God through prayer, worship, and studying His word, we can experience the reality of these promises in our lives.

Psalm 91 is a psalm that encourages greater closeness to God. It reminds us of His protection and care for us, and it encourages us to trust in Him in the midst of life's uncertainties. As we dwell in the shelter of

God's presence and declare our trust in Him, we can experience the peace, rest, and protection that only He can provide.

One of the reasons why Psalm 91 encourages greater closeness to God is because it reminds us of the importance of our relationship with Him. The psalmist declares that those who dwell in the shelter of the Most High will find rest and security under His protection. This speaks to the deep longing we all have for security and safety, and it reminds us that only in God can we find true peace and rest for our souls.

Furthermore, Psalm 91 encourages us to rely on God's strength and power instead of our own. The psalmist declares that God will protect us from the snares of the enemy, and that we will not fear the terror of the night or the arrow that flies by day. This reminds us that we do not have to face life's challenges and difficulties on our own, but that we can rely on God's strength and power to overcome them.

Another reason why Psalm 91 encourages greater closeness to God is because it reminds us of His faithfulness. The psalmist declares that God will be with us in times of trouble and that He will deliver us and honor us. This speaks to God's character as a faithful and loving Father who will never abandon us or leave us alone.

As we meditate on the promises of Psalm 91 and draw closer to God, we can experience a deeper sense of intimacy with Him. We can find rest and security in His presence, and we can trust in His faithfulness to guide us through life's challenges. Moreover, we can find comfort in the knowledge that we are not alone, but that God is with us every step of the way.

Psalm 91 is a psalm that encourages greater closeness to God. It reminds us of His protection, strength, and faithfulness, and it encourages us to trust in Him in the midst of life's uncertainties. As we draw closer to God through prayer, worship, and studying His word, we can experience the reality of His promises in our lives and find rest and security in His presence.

Another way that Psalm 91 encourages greater closeness to God is by reminding us of the importance of our faith. The psalmist declares that those who trust in God will not be afraid of the terror of the night or the arrow that flies by day. This speaks to the power of our faith in God to give us courage and strength in the face of danger and adversity.

Furthermore, Psalm 91 encourages us to see God as our refuge and fortress. The psalmist declares that God will cover us with His feathers and under His wings we will find refuge. This imagery reminds us of the tender care and protection that God provides for His children, and it encourages us to draw near to Him in times of trouble.

Another way that Psalm 91 encourages greater closeness to God is by reminding us of the power of our words. The psalmist declares that those who declare God's protection and trust in His name will experience His care and deliverance. This reminds us of the importance of speaking positive and faith-filled words, and it encourages us to declare God's promises over our lives.

Moreover, Psalm 91 encourages us to see God as our provider. The psalmist declares that God will satisfy us with long life and show us His salvation. This speaks to the abundant blessings that God provides for His children, and it encourages us to trust in His provision for our lives.

Psalm 91 is a psalm that encourages greater closeness to God in many ways. It reminds us of the importance of our faith, encourages us to see God as our refuge and fortress, reminds us of the power of our words, and encourages us to trust in God's provision for our lives. As we draw closer to God through prayer, worship, and studying His word, we can experience the fullness of His love and care for us, and find rest and security in His presence.

Another way that Psalm 91 encourages greater closeness to God is by reminding us of the power of His angels. The psalmist declares that God will command His angels to guard us in all our ways, and that they will lift us up in their hands so that we will not strike our foot against a stone. This speaks to the supernatural protection that God provides for His children, and it encourages us to trust in His divine intervention in our lives.

Furthermore, Psalm 91 encourages us to see God as our deliverer. The psalmist declares that God will deliver us from the snare of the fowler and from deadly diseases. This speaks to the power of God to rescue us from all kinds of dangers and afflictions, and it encourages us to trust in His saving power.

Another way that Psalm 91 encourages greater closeness to God is by reminding us of the importance of worship. The psalmist declares that those who love God will call upon His name, and that He will answer them and be with them in trouble. This speaks to the power of worship to connect us with God and to bring us into His presence. As we worship Him, we draw closer to Him and experience His love and care for us in a deeper way.

Moreover, Psalm 91 encourages us to see God as our protector. The psalmist declares that God will cover us with His feathers and His wings, and that we will find refuge in His shadow. This speaks to the protective care that God provides for His children, and it encourages us to trust in His ability to shield us from harm.

Psalm 91 is a psalm that encourages greater closeness to God in many ways. It reminds us of the power of God's angels, encourages us to see Him as our deliverer and protector, reminds us of the importance of worship, and encourages us to trust in His supernatural intervention in our lives. As we draw closer to God through prayer, worship, and studying His word, we can experience the fullness of His love and care for us, and find rest and security in His presence.

Sufficient Grace

God's protection is an act of God's grace. God's grace is an incredible and powerful concept that can have a profound impact on our lives. When we experience God's grace, we are given something that we do not deserve - forgiveness, love, mercy, and so much more. But perhaps the most incredible aspect of God's grace is that it is always sufficient.

This means that no matter what we are facing in life, no matter how difficult or overwhelming our circumstances may seem, God's grace is always enough to see us through. When we are weak, His strength is made perfect in us. When we are struggling, He is there to guide us and give us the courage to keep going. When we are lost, He is there to lead us back to the right path.

God's grace is not something that we can earn or deserve - it is a gift freely given to us by God, and it is available to all who seek it. Whether we are struggling with addiction, grief, anxiety, or any other challenge, God's grace is always there to offer us hope and help us overcome.

One of the most inspiring examples of God's grace in action can be found in the life of the apostle Paul. Paul was a man who had persecuted and even killed Christians before he had a powerful encounter with Jesus Christ on the road to Damascus. After this experience, Paul became one of the most influential figures in the early Christian church, writing much of the New Testament and spreading the message of God's grace to countless people.

Despite all of the trials and tribulations that Paul faced - including persecution, imprisonment, and even shipwrecks - he never lost sight of the fact that God's grace was always sufficient. In 2 Corinthians 12:9, Paul writes, "But he said to me, 'My grace is sufficient for you, for my power is made perfect in weakness.' Therefore I will boast all the more gladly about my weaknesses, so that Christ's power may rest on me."

This passage reminds us that no matter what we are facing, we can find strength in God's grace. His power is made perfect in our weakness, and His grace is always enough to see us through. So if you are feeling overwhelmed or uncertain today, remember that God's grace is available to you. Seek Him, trust Him, and allow His grace to guide you through whatever challenges may come your way.

One of the amazing things about God's grace is that it is not limited by our mistakes, failures, or shortcomings. No matter what we have done in the past, God's grace is always available to us in the present. We simply need to ask for it and receive it with a humble and contrite heart.

In fact, God's grace is often most powerful when we recognize our own weakness and turn to Him for help. This is because when we acknowledge our own limitations and depend on God's strength, we become more open to His guidance and more receptive to His blessings.

Another beautiful aspect of God's grace is that it is not just about forgiveness, but also about transformation. When we receive God's grace, we are not only forgiven of our sins, but we are also given the power to overcome them and become more like Christ. As we grow in our relationship with God, His grace transforms us from the inside out, making us more loving, compassionate, and joyful.

Ultimately, God's grace is a reflection of His great love for us. It is an undeserved gift that we can never earn or repay, but that we can freely receive and share with others. When we experience God's grace in our own lives, we are empowered to extend that same grace to others, showing love and kindness even to those who may not deserve it.

So if you are feeling overwhelmed or discouraged today, remember that God's grace is always sufficient. Turn to Him in prayer, and trust that His grace will guide you through whatever challenges you may face. And as you experience the transforming power of His grace in your life, be sure to share that same grace with others, spreading His love and light wherever you go.

One of the most beautiful aspects of God's grace is that it is not just a one-time event, but rather a continuous flow of love and mercy in our lives. As we grow in our relationship with God, we can experience His grace in new and deeper ways, strengthening our faith and helping us to become more like Christ.

God's grace can be seen in every aspect of our lives, from the beauty of nature to the kindness of strangers. It is a reminder that we are not alone in this world, and that there is a loving God who cares for us and provides for our needs.

Moreover, God's grace is not just for our benefit, but also for the benefit of others. As we receive God's grace, we are called to extend that same grace to others, showing love and compassion to those who may be struggling or hurting. This is the heart of the Christian message, and it is a powerful testimony to the world of the transformative power of God's grace.

In the book of Ephesians, the apostle Paul writes, "For it is by grace you have been saved, through faith—and this is not from yourselves, it is the gift of God—not by works, so that no one can boast" (Ephesians 2:8-9). This passage reminds us that God's grace is a gift that we cannot earn or deserve, but that we can freely receive through faith in Jesus Christ.

As we continue to walk in faith and receive God's grace in our lives, we can have confidence that His grace is always sufficient. No matter what challenges or obstacles we may face, we can trust in God's love and mercy to guide us through and help us overcome. And as we extend that same grace to others, we can

185

become agents of transformation and hope in a world that desperately needs it.

Another aspect of God's grace that is truly remarkable is that it is available to everyone, regardless of who they are or what they have done. God's grace is not limited to a select few who have lived perfect lives, but rather is offered to all who are willing to receive it.

This is seen in the life of the apostle Paul, who before his encounter with Christ was known for his persecution of Christians. Yet even in the midst of his sin and rebellion, God's grace was able to reach him and transform his life. Paul would go on to become one of the greatest advocates for God's grace, writing in his letter to Timothy, "Here is a trustworthy saying that deserves full acceptance: Christ Jesus came into the world to save sinners—of whom I am the worst" (1 Timothy 1:15).

Paul's story is a powerful reminder that God's grace is not just for the righteous or the deserving, but for all who are willing to turn to Him in repentance and faith. No matter how far we may have strayed from God's path, His grace is always available to lead us back to Him.

In addition, God's grace is not just about forgiveness, but also about restoration. Through His grace, God is able to take even the most broken and damaged parts of our lives and transform them into something beautiful. As we surrender our lives to Him and allow His grace to work in us, we can become the people that He created us to be, living out our purpose and fulfilling His plan for our lives.

So if you are feeling lost, broken, or in need of direction, know that God's grace is always sufficient. Turn to Him in prayer, and trust that His love and mercy will guide you through whatever challenges you may face. And as you experience His transforming grace in your life, be sure to share that same grace with others, offering hope and healing to all who are in need.

Greek is an important language in Christianity as it was the language in which the New Testament was originally written. The apostles and early Christian leaders communicated in Greek, and the language was used to spread the Christian message throughout the Mediterranean world.

In fact, the New Testament uses two different forms of Greek - Koine Greek, which was the common language of the people, and Classical Greek, which was a more formal and academic form of the language. The use of both forms of Greek helped to make the teachings of Christianity accessible to a wide audience, from the educated elites to the common people.

Some of the most important theological concepts in Christianity are also expressed in Greek, such as the term "charis," which means grace. This word is used throughout the New Testament to describe the unmerited favor and mercy of God that is available to all who believe in Him. The Apostle Paul, who wrote many of the New Testament letters, used the Greek word "charis" extensively to describe the transformative power of God's grace in the lives of believers. Overall, Greek has played a significant role in the development and spread of Christianity, and continues to be studied and used in theological and scholarly circles today.

Psalm 91 is a beautiful and powerful testament to God's amazing grace. The psalm begins with a declaration of trust in God's protection and provision, proclaiming, "He who dwells in the secret place of the Most High shall abide under the shadow of the Almighty" (Psalm 91:1).

Throughout the psalm, we see the many ways in which God's grace is available to those who trust in Him. We are told that God will protect us from deadly diseases and dangers, that He will shield us from harm and provide for our needs. But perhaps the most incredible aspect of God's grace illustrated in Psalm 91 is the promise of eternal life and salvation.

In verse 14, God speaks directly to the psalmist, declaring, "Because he has set his love upon Me, therefore I will deliver him; I will set him on high, because he has known My name." This verse illustrates that our salvation is not based on our own merit or works, but rather on our faith and trust in God. When we set our love upon Him and know His name, He promises to deliver us and set us on high, giving us eternal life and the hope of glory.

The final verses of Psalm 91 are a powerful affirmation of God's faithfulness and protection. We are told that God will be with us in times of trouble, that He will rescue us and honor us, and that He will give us long life and satisfy us with His salvation.

Overall, Psalm 91 is a beautiful illustration of God's amazing grace. It reminds us that no matter what challenges or dangers we may face in this life, we can trust in God's protection and provision. His grace is sufficient to see us through, and His love and mercy are available to all who trust in Him. As we meditate on this psalm and on the many promises of God's grace contained within it, may we be encouraged and strengthened in our faith, knowing that He who has promised is faithful to fulfill His word.

One of the most incredible aspects of Psalm 91 is the way in which it reminds us of the intimate and personal relationship we can have with God. The psalmist speaks of God in deeply personal terms, referring to Him as "my refuge and my fortress," and declaring, "He shall call upon Me, and I will answer him; I will be with him in trouble; I will deliver him and honor him" (Psalm 91:2, 15).

This language of intimacy and relationship reminds us that God's grace is not just an abstract concept, but rather a real and tangible force in our lives. Through His grace, we can experience a deep and abiding relationship with Him, in which we are protected, guided, and loved beyond measure.

Psalm 91 illustrates the way in which God's grace is available to us in all circumstances. Whether we are facing trials and tribulations, or enjoying times of peace and prosperity, God's grace is there to sustain us and see us through.

This is seen in verses 7 and 8, which declare, "A thousand may fall at your side, and ten thousand at your right hand; but it shall not come near you. Only with your eyes shall you look, and see the reward of the wicked."

These verses remind us that no matter how dire our circumstances may seem, God's grace is always sufficient to protect us and keep us safe. We may see others around us falling or suffering, but we can trust in God's promise that He will never leave us or forsake us.

Ultimately, Psalm 91 is a testament to the incredible power of God's grace in our lives. It reminds us that His grace is not just a distant or abstract concept, but rather a real and tangible force that is available to us in all circumstances. May we always be mindful of God's grace, and may we trust in His promises to protect and provide for us, both now and forevermore.

Understanding Secret Places

Psalm 91 is a beautiful and powerful passage of Scripture that speaks about the protection and provision of God. One of the most intriguing parts of this Psalm is the reference to "secret places". In verse 1, the Psalmist declares, "He who dwells in the secret place of the Most High shall abide under the shadow of the Almighty."

What does it mean to dwell in the secret place of the Most High? The secret place is not a physical location, but rather a spiritual reality. It is a place of intimacy and closeness with God. It is a place where we can find refuge and rest in the midst of life's storms. It is a place where we can receive guidance and direction from the Lord.

The secret place is a place of safety and security. When we dwell in this place, we are under the protection of the Almighty. We are shielded from harm and danger. We can trust in God's faithfulness and His ability to keep us safe.

But the secret place is also a place of provision. In verse 2, the Psalmist says, "I will say of the Lord, 'He is my refuge and my fortress; my God, in Him I will trust.'" When we trust in God and make Him our refuge and fortress, He provides for our every need. He meets our physical, emotional, and spiritual needs.

So, how do we dwell in the secret place of the Most High? The answer is found in verse 14: "Because he has set his love upon Me, therefore I will deliver him; I will set him on high, because he has known My name." We must set our love upon God and know His name. We must cultivate a deep and abiding relationship with Him through prayer, worship, and the study of His Word.

Psalm 91 teaches us that the secret place of the Most High is a place of safety, security, and provision. It is a place where we can find rest, guidance, and direction. It is a place where we can experience the love and faithfulness of God. May we all strive to dwell in this secret place and trust in the protection and provision of our Heavenly Father.

The concept of the secret place in Psalm 91 is also closely related to the idea of the "shadow of the Almighty" mentioned in the same verse. The shadow of the Almighty is a metaphorical expression for the presence of God, which provides shelter and protection for His people. It is interesting to note that shadows are created when an object blocks the light from a source. In the same way, when we are in the shadow of the Almighty, it is because we are positioned behind Him, with Him in front of us, blocking any harm that may come our way.

Another important aspect of the secret place is that it is a place of rest. In verse 1, the Psalmist says that those who dwell in the secret place shall "abide under the shadow of the Almighty". The word "abide" here means to dwell, to remain, or to stay. This implies a sense of permanence and stability, which is the opposite of being restless and anxious. When we are in the secret place, we can rest in the assurance of God's protection and provision, knowing that He is in control of all things.

Moreover, the secret place is not only a place of protection and provision, but also a place of transformation. In verse 15, God says, "He shall call upon Me, and I will answer him; I will be with him in trouble; I will deliver him and honor him." When we call upon God in the secret place, He responds by delivering us and honoring us. This process of deliverance and honor involves transformation, as we are changed into the image of Christ through the trials and challenges that we face.

Finally, the secret place is a place of intimacy. In verse 14, God says, "Because he has set his love upon Me, therefore I will deliver him." The secret place is not just a physical or spiritual location, but a state of being in a close and intimate relationship with God. When we set our love upon God, He responds by drawing us close to Himself and revealing Himself to us in new and deeper ways.

The secret place in Psalm 91 is a powerful metaphor for the protection, provision, rest, transformation, and intimacy that we can experience in our relationship with God. May we all strive to dwell in this secret place, seeking after Him with all our hearts, and trusting in His love and faithfulness.

Psalm 91 was originally written in Hebrew and that the phrase "secret place" in verse 1 is translated from the Hebrew word "sether" which can also mean "a hiding place" or "a covering." The word "sether" implies a sense of protection and concealment, suggesting that the secret place is a place of safety and security.

Additionally, the phrase "shadow of the Almighty" in verse 1 is translated from the Hebrew word "tsel" which can also mean "shade" or "protection." The word "tsel" is often used in the Old Testament to describe the protection and provision that God offers His people.

Furthermore, the word "abide" in verse 1 is translated from the Hebrew word "yashab" which can also mean "to dwell" or "to remain." The word "yashab" connotes a sense of permanence and stability, indicating that those who dwell in the secret place will experience a lasting sense of safety and security.

While the New Testament was written in Greek, there are no direct references to the secret place in the New Testament. However, the concept of the secret place is closely related to the idea of abiding in Christ, which is mentioned in John 15:4-5. In these verses, Jesus says, "Abide in Me, and I in you. As the branch cannot bear fruit of itself, unless it abides in the vine, neither can you, unless you abide in Me. I am the vine, you are the branches. He who abides in Me, and

I in him, bears much fruit; for without Me you can do nothing."

The idea of abiding in Christ is similar to the concept of dwelling in the secret place. Both involve a deep and abiding relationship with God, characterized by trust, intimacy, and dependence. Both also offer protection, provision, and transformation, as we draw closer to God and become more like Him.

While the original Hebrew, Greek, and Aramaic languages provide deeper insights into the meaning of Psalm 91, the concept of the secret place is universal and applicable to all believers, regardless of their language or cultural background. May we all seek to dwell in the secret place of the Most High, trusting in His protection, provision, and transformative power.

Another interesting aspect of the language used in Psalm 91 is the use of metaphors to describe the protection and provision that God offers. In addition to the "secret place" and the "shadow of the Almighty," the Psalmist also uses other images to convey the idea of safety and security. For example, in verse 4, he says, "He shall cover you with His feathers, and under His wings you shall take refuge." This metaphor of a bird protecting its young under its wings is a powerful image of God's care and tenderness towards His people.

Similarly, in verse 12, the Psalmist speaks of God's angels as being "charged over you, to keep you in all your ways." This imagery of angelic protection is a common theme in the Bible, and it emphasizes the supernatural dimension of God's protection.

Furthermore, the use of the word "deliver" in Psalm 91 is significant. In the original Hebrew, the word used for "deliver" is "natsal," which can also mean "to snatch away" or "to rescue." This word implies a sense of urgency and action on God's part, suggesting that He is actively working to protect His people from harm.

It is worth noting that the language used in Psalm 91 is not just descriptive, but also prescriptive. That is, the Psalmist is not just describing the protection and provision that God offers, but also encouraging the reader to take action to receive these benefits. In verse 9, for example, he says, "Because you have made the Lord, who is my refuge, even the Most High, your dwelling place." This verse implies that we have a choice to make - we can choose to make God our dwelling place, and in so doing, we can experience His protection and provision.

The language used in Psalm 91 provides a rich and nuanced understanding of God's protection and provision for His people. Through metaphors, imagery, and prescriptive language, the Psalmist conveys the idea that God is a powerful and loving protector who offers safety, security, and transformation to those who seek refuge in Him. May we all take comfort in the language of Psalm 91 and trust in God's care and provision for our lives.

One interesting aspect of the language used in Psalm 91 is the repetition of the word "He" throughout the Psalm. This word is used to refer to God, and it serves to emphasize His power, sovereignty, and faithfulness. By using the pronoun "He" instead of a more specific name or title for God, the Psalmist emphasizes the all-encompassing nature of God's protection and provision. God is not just a provider of physical or material needs, but a source of protection and security in all areas of life.

Another significant aspect of the language in Psalm 91 is the use of conditional language. Throughout the Psalm, the blessings of God's protection and provision are linked to certain conditions, such as trust, obedience, and love. In verse 14, for example, God says, "Because he has set his love upon Me, therefore I will deliver him." This verse implies that our love for God is a prerequisite for receiving His protection and provision.

Furthermore, the language in Psalm 91 is not just descriptive and prescriptive, but also emotive. The Psalmist uses strong and vivid language to convey the depth of God's care and concern for His people. In verse 3, he says, "Surely He shall deliver you from the snare of the fowler and from the perilous pestilence." The use of the word "surely" here implies a sense of certainty and conviction, indicating the

Psalmist's deep trust in God's power and faithfulness.

Similarly, in verse 7, he says, "A thousand may fall at your side, and ten thousand at your right hand; but it shall not come near you." This verse uses hyperbole to emphasize the extent of God's protection. Even in the midst of great danger and calamity, God's people can trust in His provision and care.

The language used in Psalm 91 is rich and multi-layered, conveying a deep and abiding sense of God's protection and provision for His people. Through the use of metaphors, imagery, conditional language, and emotive language, the Psalmist emphasizes the all-encompassing nature of God's care and the importance of trust, obedience, and love. May we all take comfort in the language of Psalm 91 and trust in God's provision and protection for our lives.

# The Angelic Realms

The testimony I received still stirs me to this day. The rain fell in sheets as Jenna stumbled through the deserted city streets, her feet splashing in puddles and her hair clinging to her face. She had been out for a walk when the storm had hit, and now she was lost and alone.

The wind howled through the empty buildings, making Jenna shiver with cold and fear. She clutched her coat tightly around her and tried to find her way back home, but the rain was so heavy she couldn't see more than a few feet in front of her.

As she stumbled down a deserted alleyway, Jenna suddenly heard a soft fluttering sound.

She looked up and saw a shimmering figure descending from the sky, its wings beating slowly and gracefully.

Jenna gasped in amazement as the figure landed beside her, its wings folding neatly behind it. She couldn't believe what she was seeing - an angel, right here in front of her.

"Are you lost, child?" the angel asked, its voice like the sweetest music.

Jenna nodded, unable to find her voice. The angel smiled kindly and took her hand, leading her out of the alleyway and onto the main street.

Together they walked through the storm, the angel shielding Jenna with its wings and guiding her through the darkness. The wind and rain lashed against them, but they were protected by a warm and comforting light that seemed to emanate from the angel's very being.

As they walked, Jenna felt a sense of peace and safety that she had never known before. She knew that no matter what happened, she was protected by this angel, and nothing could harm her.

Finally, they reached Jenna's doorstep, and the angel bid her farewell with a gentle touch of its hand. As Jenna watched it ascend back into the sky, she felt a sense of gratitude and wonder that stayed with her long after the storm had passed.

From that day on, Jenna knew that she was never truly alone. She had been protected by an angel, and that knowledge gave her the courage to face whatever challenges lay ahead.

Belief in the existence of angels has been a part of human culture and spirituality for thousands of years. Across different religions and cultures, people have shared stories and beliefs about beings that are divine messengers, guardians, and protectors.

While angels are often associated with the teachings of Abrahamic religions like Christianity, Judaism, and Islam, the concept of celestial beings has also appeared in other ancient cultures. In Hinduism, for example, the devas and asuras are celestial beings with god-like powers, while the ancient Greeks and Romans believed in the existence of guardian spirits or daimons.

Despite the differences in these beliefs, what remains consistent is the idea that these beings are benevolent and can offer guidance, protection, and support to humans. This belief in the existence of angels can bring comfort and hope to those who hold it, particularly during times of struggle and hardship.

For many, the existence of angels is not a matter of faith alone but also of personal experience. People have reported encountering angelic beings in moments of crisis, whether through visions, dreams, or unexplainable occurrences. These experiences can be profound and life-changing, and often inspire individuals to strengthen their faith and trust in the existence of angels.

Furthermore, belief in angels can also inspire acts of kindness and compassion towards others. Knowing that there are celestial beings watching over and guiding us can give us a sense of purpose and responsibility to help those in need, to be kind, and to spread love.

# ABOUT THE AUTHOR

Dr. Jeremy Lopez is Founder and President of Identity Network and Now Is Your Moment. Identity Network is one of the world's leading prophetic resource sites, offering books, teachings, and courses to a global audience. For more than thirty years, Dr. Lopez has been considered a pioneering voice within the field of the prophetic arts and his proven strategies for success coaching are now being implemented by various training groups and faith groups throughout the world. Dr. Lopez is the author of more than forty books, including his international bestselling books The Universe is at Your Command and Creating with Your Thoughts. Throughout his career, he has spoken prophetically into the lives of heads of business as well as heads of state. He has ministered to Governor Bob Riley of the State of Alabama, Prime Minister Benjamin Netanyahu, and Shimon Peres. Dr. Lopez continues to be a highly sought conference teacher and host, speaking on the topics of human potential and spirituality.